TRAVELING ROUTE 66

TRAVELING ROUTE 66

Nick Freeth

Consulting Editor: Paul Taylor,
Publisher of *Route 66 Magazine*

**University of Oklahoma Press
Norman**

4 CREDITS

Consulting editor:
Paul Taylor, *Route 66 Magazine*
Editor: Philip de Ste. Croix
Design and page make-up:
Philip Clucas MSIAD
Photography:
Dan Harlow, Neil Sutherland

Editorial Director: Will Steeds
Production: Neil Randles
Color reproduction: Pica Colour
Separations (Pte) Ltd, Singapore
Printed and bound: Star Standard
Industries (Pte) Ltd, Singapore

Oklahoma Paperbacks edition published 2001 by the University of Oklahoma Press, Norman, Publishing Division of the University, by special arrangement with Salamander Books Ltd., 8 Blenheim Court, Brewery Road, London N7 9NT, United Kingdom.

All correspondence concerning the content of this volume should be addressed to Salamander Books Ltd.

The majority of the photographs of locations along Route 66 published in this book were supplied by the photographer Dan Harlow to whom the publishers extend warm thanks for his help and encouragement.

1 2 3 4 5 6 7 8 9 10

Library of Congress Cataloging-in-Publication Data
Freeth, Nick, 1956–
 Traveling Route 66/Nick Freeth; consulting editor, Paul Taylor.
  p. cm.
 Includes bibliographical references and index.
 ISBN 0-8061-3326-0 (pbk.: alk. paper)
 1. United States Highway 66—History. 2. West (U. S.)—Description and travel. I. Taylor, Paul, 1931– II. Title.

HE356.W37F73 2001
917.304'929—dc21   00-048005

The information in this book is true and complete to the best of our knowledge. All recommendations are made without any guarantee on the part of the author or publisher, who also disclaim any liability incurred in connection with the use of this data or specific details.

Nick Freeth was born in London in 1956. After graduating from St. Catharine's College, Cambridge with a degree in English Literature, he joined the BBC in 1978, and later became a senior producer in the World Service, where he specialized in making radio programs covering folk, jazz, and blues. Nick left the BBC in 1990 to work as Senior Producer for the London radio station Jazz FM, producing the 26-part series "100 Years of Jazz" and a wide range of other shows. In 1992, he was appointed Head of Music Production at Rewind Productions, an independent company making radio programs for the BBC. In 1994, Nick and his colleague Charles Alexander formed their own production company, Gleneagle Productions, whose recent radio commissions have included a 12-part survey of "The Guitar in Jazz," and a series examining the history of jazz in Nazi Germany. He is the author, with Charles Alexander, of *The Acoustic Guitar* and *The Electric Guitar*.

ROUTE
66

Contents

Introduction by Paul Taylor

Just when you think that you have seen every book that chronicles the spirit of Route 66, along comes another celebration of the historic highway. You are holding in your hands the newest offering to the Mother Road—a state-by-state Route 66 odyssey authored by English journalist Nick Freeth. And it is obvious that Nick knows the mystique and excitement of Route 66, as he so aptly captures the mood and magic that has made the old cross-country route the world's most nostalgic highway. Don't be fooled by this small package—within its pages is a colorful, illustrated history of the fabled road and its landmarks.

Traveling Route 66 is packed with memories of my teen years in the late 1940s, when the family got together at the table and plotted a course that would take us on vacation across U.S. Highway 66.

Gasoline was 17¢ a gallon. Haircuts were 25¢. A set of Allstate clincher tires was $43.80 — installed. We paid 35¢ toll to cross the Chain of Rocks Bridge over the Mississippi River. We filled our water bag in Tulsa, and wondered who was crazy enough to bury those Cadillacs nose first in the ground outside of Amarillo, Texas.

The fabled ribbon of asphalt and concrete still winds her way across the country, and this handy book is your passport to the sights and sounds of America's Main Street.

Prologue

Route 66 is the USA's most famous highway. Opened in 1926, it connected Chicago with Los Angeles, over 2,000 miles (3,200km) to the southwest, and made long-distance road transportation a reality for millions of Americans. It played a key role in the development of industry and commerce, offered the prospect of a new, better life in the West for families trapped in rural poverty along its path, and gave vital support to the US war effort in the 1940s. And it quickly became part of the American Dream, generating its own myths and romance, and inspiring scores of novelists, poets, artists, moviemakers, and songwriters to weave its images into their work. This book follows the path of the Mother Road, assesses its importance, and attempts, in the process, to capture something of its special magic.

Right: Winslow, Arizona — one of hundreds of small towns that benefited from Route 66.

By the 1920s, America's railroads boasted over 200,000 miles (320,000km) of operational track. The country's road system was far less advanced; but an increase in car ownership, as well

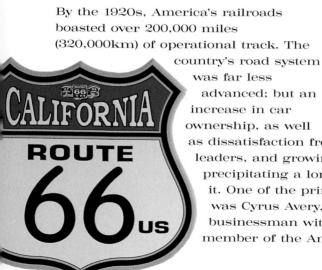

as dissatisfaction from state and business leaders, and growing Federal investment, was precipitating a long-overdue improvement in it. One of the prime movers in this process was Cyrus Avery, an Oklahoma-based businessman with a passion for roads. As a member of the American Association of State

Highway Officials, he wished to see the existing, haphazardly organized system of "named" roads (like the Lincoln Highway and National Old Trails Highway) replaced by an integrated network of interstate routes. One of his ideas was for an east-west thoroughfare from Chicago to California, taking in his own home state; this road was formally proposed in October 1925, and approved, allocated a "route" number — 66 — and opened by the following year.

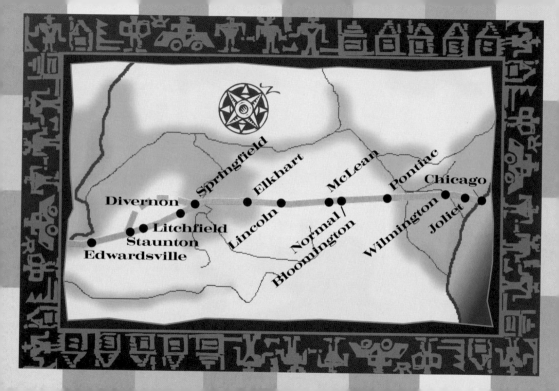

Illinois

In the early 1830s, much of Illinois was prairie, and Chicago was just a marshy, sparsely inhabited settlement on the edge of Lake Michigan. By the following decade, however, Chicago had become an important hub for the transportation of crops and livestock by ship; and the coming of the railroads established it, in the words of Alistair Cooke, as "the ideal junction between the harvests of the encircling prairie and the people who would eat and use them." Route 66 opened up the prospect of reliable long-distance road freight to and from Chicago, and its 290-mile (467km) long Illinois section, leading southwest towards the Mississippi, was already fully paved before the highway's inauguration in 1926.

ILLINOIS

ILLINOIS

Landscape & Climate

Chicago got its nickname, the "windy city," from the bitter Arctic air that blows in across Lake Michigan. At its coldest, in January, average temperatures in the area can fall to 18°F (-8°C); the summer maximum is around 86°F (30°C). The fertile prairie land covering much of the state of Illinois is now mostly under cultivation: the region's main crops are corn, soyabeans, and oats; and — appropriately — its major industries include the manufacture of farm machinery. Route 66 heads southwest from Chicago via the state capital, Springfield, to the plains surrounding the Mississippi River — the lowest-lying part of Illinois, standing less than 300 feet (91m) above sea-level.

If you ever plan to motor west;

Travel my way, take the highway that's the best.

Get your kicks on Route Sixty-Six!

It winds from Chicago to L.A.,

More than two thousand miles all the way.

Get your kicks on Route Sixty-Six!

(from Route 66 by Bobby Troup, 1946)

The sign bearing the words "Start of Historic Route 66" is at the junction of Adams Street and Michigan Avenue. However, at the time of its inauguration in 1926, much of the highway remained unpaved, and long-distance road travel was feasible only for the most adventurous drivers and sturdiest vehicles. Railroads, in contrast, already had well-established tracks and an impressive downtown base — the famous Union Station, sited on Jackson Boulevard, close to Adams and Michigan. Opened in 1925, it offered an easily accessible gateway to an extensive range of destinations, and its imposing appearance seems to symbolize the railroad's long-assumed superiority to roads. Eventually, of course, trains were to lose much of their business to automobiles and trucks on 66 and its Interstate successors — but the many miles of railtrack running alongside the highway in Illinois and other states on the journey west are a continual reminder of their former significance.

Right: Two views of the Windy City and (below inset) journey's end at Santa Monica.

Night Scene, Looking South, on Michigan Boulevard, Chicago

SM-44 A GENERAL VIEW OF SANTA MONICA, CALIF.

SHOWING YACHT HARBOR, THE PALISADES, AND THE SANTA MONICA MOUNTAINS IN THE DISTANCE

Chicago is famous for its commerce, its architecture (the first skyscrapers were built there), and its music — but also for the activities of Al Capone (1899—1947), who controlled organized crime, prostitution, and the supply of illicit alcohol in the city for much of the 1920s. His headquarters — the New Michigan, a former hotel on Michigan Avenue — is worth making a detour to see before starting the long journey southwest.

Ogden Avenue provides the route out of central Chicago, leading towards the districts of Cicero and Berwyn. The highway continues via Harlem Avenue and Joliet Road to I-55, where the traveler can either stay on the Interstate, following the more direct southwesterly path taken by 66 after 1940, or turn off at exit 269 to explore its original alignment. This leads through the towns of Joliet (whose Stateville Prison was immortalized in *The Blues Brothers*), Elwood, and Wilmington.

Left: The New Michigan Hotel on Chicago's Michigan Avenue — headquarters of the crime syndicate led by Al "Scarface" Capone.

The Launching Pad Café

On a pedestal outside Wilmington's Launching Pad restaurant stands the 20-foot (6m) tall "Gemini Giant," resplendent in his green space suit and huge helmet, and cradling a toy rocket in his hands. The Giant, which has been there since the Launching Pad opened for business in the early 1960s, is one of three similar statues (all made by the same Californian fiber-glass company) to be seen on Route 66 in Illinois. The others adorn a drive-in near Cicero and an auto supply store in Springfield.

*Left: Gas station
in Odell —
opened in 1932
and originally
run by Standard
before becoming
a Sinclair outlet.*

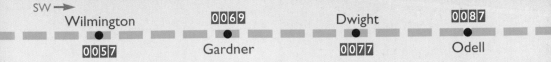

SW →

Wilmington

`0069`

Dwight

`0087`

`0057`

Gardner

`0077`

Odell

The development of Route 66 and other highways led to the rapid growth of many new roadside facilities. One of the most significant of these was the service station, owned or franchised by regional and national oil companies, and providing easy access to gas, water, and other essentials. According to Jerry McClanahan, writing in *Route 66 Magazine*, the first ever gas pumps were used by the Automobile Gasoline Company of St. Louis, Missouri, in 1905; previously, drivers had often had to fill their vehicles from buckets. Modern-style service stations with underground fuel tanks had appeared by 1913; the first one on Route 66 was probably Shell's outlet at Mount Olive, Illinois, which opened in 1926. The Maraton Oil Station at Dwight, just over 20 miles (32km) west of Wilmington, has been in business since 1932, and the Sinclair station in nearby Odell (illustrated here; it was later taken over by Phillips and subsequently by Sinclair) dates from the same period.

The town of Pontiac, ten miles (16km) west of Odell, gave its name to the original Chicago-St. Louis road, the Pontiac Trail, whose path through Illinois is broadly followed by Route 66. The barn shown opposite, advertising Missouri's Meramec Caverns (which are featured on pages 80-81) can be seen on the right of the highway outside the town.

About 30 miles (48km) west of Pontiac, beyond Chenoa, Lexington, and Towanda, are Normal and Bloomington, which share the same Main Street. It was here, in 1934, that Gus Belt founded the first of his famous "Steak 'n' Shake" restaurants, where the raw meat was ground into burgers in front of the customers, and the machines mixing the milkshakes were positioned in the windows to attract passing motorists. Gus Belt died in 1954, but his restaurant in Normal continues to thrive, and there are currently over 300 other "Steak 'n' Shake" outlets all over the USA.

Left: An advertisement outside Pontiac for Missouri's Meramec Caverns – more than 250 miles (400km) to the southwest!

Although the 20 horsepower, $325 Super-X was a relatively short-lived model, its design made a great impact on the American motorcycle industry.

1930 Excelsior Super X

The early days of Route 66 coincided with the last great years of the Chicago-based Excelsior motorcycle company — one of the trio of major manufacturers (together with Indian and Harley-Davidson) who dominated the industry throughout the Roaring Twenties.

Excelsior's 750cc Super-X, launched in 1925, was an immediate success; with a top speed of 65mph (105kph), it outperformed many larger machines. It remained in production until Excelsior went out of business during the Depression.

Left: The Super-X proved itself in off-road racing, where it often outperformed larger machines.

After leaving Bloomington and Normal, 66 passes through Funks Grove — a settlement surrounded by maple trees, named for the Funk family who have lived there since the 1820s. The Funks are among the longest established commercial producers of maple sirup, and a good deal of what they make is now sold by mail order or shipped overseas. However, as Steve Funk (whose great-grandfather, Issac, was one of the first inhabitants of the Grove) explained to Route 66

Right: Three happy customers outside the Dixie Trucker's Home in McLean.

expert Michael Wallis, "We've
always sold sirup right off the
back porch. People know Funks
Grove sirup is a sign that spring
is just around the corner. We still
have regular customers from St.
Louis to Chicago."

Perhaps some of that Funks
Grove sirup finds its way to the
Dixie Trucker's Home in nearby
McLean. This remarkable
institution was the first-ever
truck stop on Route 66, and
its history is outlined on the
next two pages.

ILLINOIS

ROUTE

66 US

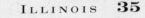

The first man to cater for the needs of Route 66's truckers — who required food and rest for themselves, as well as fuel for their vehicles — was J.P. Walters, who acquired McLean's Shirley Oil and Supply Company in 1928. He and his son-in-law, John Geske, introduced round-the-clock service to accommodate their customers' irregular hours, offering food and coffee as well as diesel and gas, and creating an atmosphere of Southern-style hospitality reflected in the name they gave their business: the Dixie Trucker's Home. Since the 1920s, four generations of the Geske family have been involved in running the Dixie, which has been closed for only one day (due to fire) in its 70-year history. It welcomes all travelers (not only truckers), provides an extensive menu of classic American food, and has the Route 66 Association of Illinois' "Hall of Fame" on permanent display near the restaurant.

Left: The distinctive Dixie Trucker's Home logo — and its menu card.

MUSIC OF THE ROAD →

In Jack Kerouac's novel *On The Road*, Sal Paradise and Dean Moriarty (alias Kerouac and his friend Neal Cassady) reach Chicago after a 17-hour drive from Denver, and spend the night enraptured by the city's impromptu jazz sessions. Chicago had been a focus for great music since the end of Word War I, thanks to an influx of migrants from Mississippi, and from the 1920s onwards, its clubs and cafés gave leading jazz artists a chance to play to mixed (black and white) audiences. Early attractions included King Oliver's Creole Jazz Band (with Louis Armstrong on second cornet); and the city soon produced star names of its own, notably clarinettist and bandleader Benny Goodman, and cornetist Jimmy McPartland. Chicago was also a magnet for musicians from further afield — like British-born pianist George Shearing, who makes a cameo appearance in *On The Road*, prompting Dean to remark to Sal that "God has arrived."

Right: Chicago has been a Mecca for jazz lovers since the 1920s.

Below: Ernie Edwards' celebrated Pig Hip Restaurant in Broadwell.

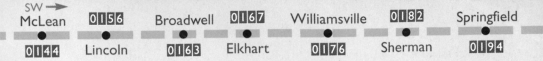

SW →
McLean 0156 Broadwell 0167 Williamsville 0182 Springfield
0144 Lincoln 0163 Elkhart 0176 Sherman 0194

A few miles south of McLean is the city of Lincoln — originally known as Postville, but renamed in 1853 in honor of Abraham Lincoln (1809—1865), who had been elected to the US House of Representatives in 1846, but was not yet a nationally-known figure. When asked to give the change his blessing, the future President self-deprecatingly remarked that he "never knew anything named Lincoln that amounted to much;" and at the subsequent public ceremony held to mark the transition, he is said to have "re-christened" the town using juice from a watermelon!

Beyond Lincoln lies Broadwell, site of the Pig Hip restaurant opened by Ernie Edwards in 1937. Once famous for its burgers and sandwiches, the Pig Hip remained in business for 54 years, and is still remembered fondly by many travelers. Thirty miles (48km) further on, the road reaches Illinois's state capital, Springfield, after passing through Elkhart, Williamsville, and Sherman.

Springfield

`0194`

Springfield is famous as the former home and final resting-place of US President Abraham Lincoln. He moved there in 1837, and met his future wife, Mary Todd, in the city two years later. From 1844 until 1861, when Lincoln was elected President, he and his family lived in a house on the corner of Eighth and Jackson; this area has been preserved and is open to visitors. After Lincoln's assassination, his body was buried in the Lincoln Tomb at the city's Oak Ridge Cemetery, and, as Michael Wallis puts it in his *Route 66 — The Mother Road*, "the whole city remains a monument to the prairie lawyer."

Right: Abraham Lincoln, Springfield's most famous resident.

Understandably, Springfield has been less pleased by the assumption that Matt Groening's notorious cartoon characters, the Simpsons, are residents of the city. However, Homer Simpson's driver's license (glimpsed in one episode of the show) reveals that he comes from "Springfield, NT" — a non-existent place not to be confused with Illinois' state capital!

Left: The growth in Route 66's popularity led to the publication of hundreds of maps and guides.

VOICE OF THE ROAD →

I am bound for the promised
land,
I'm bound for the promised
land;
O who will come and go
with me?
I am bound for the promised
land.

(Old American folk song)

In the early 1940s, Ed Waldmire, then based in Amarillo, Texas, created the corn dog — a hot dog covered in cornmeal batter, deep-fried, and served on a stick. It proved hugely successful in Amarillo, and later in Springfield, where, in 1949, Ed opened his Cozy Dog Drive In. The diner became a familiar landmark on 66, and in 1991, two years before his death, Ed Waldmire was inducted into Illinois' Route 66 Hall of Fame.

His son Bob has pursued a very different path. A skilled artist and a free spirit, he spent many years

Right: Two "dancing dogs" decorate the sign for Ed Waldmire's Cozy Drive In.

traveling 66 in a camper van, creating his distinctive "bird's-eye" maps of the highway, and drawing its animals, plants, and scenery. For several years, he ran a Route 66 visitor center in Hackberry, Arizona, but has recently returned to Springfield, and is currently working on an anthology of his father's favorite writings, which will also contain photographs, drawings, and reminiscences from Ed's family and friends.

Above: The Lincoln Motel and Dining Room — another landmark in Springfield.

Below: "Our Lady of the Highways."

ILLINOIS

Left: The inscription reads: "Mary loving Mother of Jesus protect us on the highway."

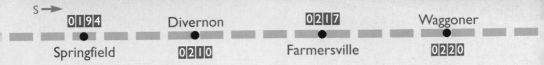

S →

| 0194 | Divernon | 0217 | Waggoner |

Springfield | 0210 | Farmersville | 0220 |

Outside Springfield, 66 originally headed west of the modern road, taking in the towns of Chatham and Carlinville before reaching Staunton. This alignment was abandoned in 1930, when the highway was re-routed in a more direct southerly path leading through Divernon, Farmersville, and Waggoner. Three miles (5km) beyond Waggoner is one of Route 66's most celebrated landmarks: a marble statue of the Virgin Mary with an inscription asking for protection for travelers. The statue, known as "Our Lady of the Highways," was crafted in Italy, and is a replica of the image of the Virgin displayed at Lourdes in France. It was erected in 1959 by a group of local Catholic Youth Organizations, and is sited on land owned by a local farmer, Francis Marten, whose daughter was one of the original fundraisers. Mr. Marten, now in his eighties, still tends the shrine regularly, and pays for the electricity that illuminates it at night.

1957 Chevrolet Bel Air

Chevrolet's '57 Bel Air belongs — like Route 66 itself — to the Golden Age of American motoring. Over 47,000 of these high-powered, budget-priced sedans were sold in less than a year.

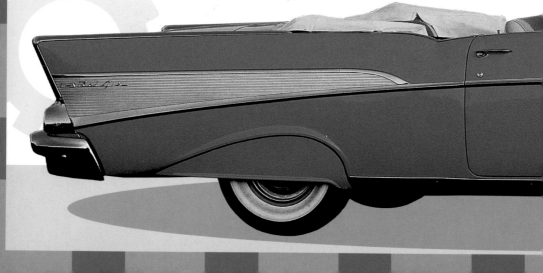

The Bel Air's sleek body and distinctive, two-tone interior were the perfect complement to its big V8 engine; top speed was 120mph (193kph).

SW →

Litchfield	0240	Staunton	0253	Edwardsville

0232   Mt. Olive   0245   Hamel   0261

The towns of Litchfield and Mt. Olive, south of the farming land around Waggoner, were once a part of southern Illinois' thriving coal industry. Although the mines are now worked out, Mt. Olive retains an important monument to its industrial past within its Union Miners' Cemetery — the Mother Jones Memorial, built in 1936 near the grave of Mary Harris Jones (1830—1930), a tireless fighter for workers' rights. Her battles with the mine bosses, together with her opposition to the exploitation of child labor, led her to be branded "the grandmother of all agitators" by one US Senator. In her eighties, she was briefly imprisoned for her activities, but she remained committed to the miners' cause until her death at the age of 99.

Beyond Mt. Olive lies Staunton; the pre- and post-1930 alignments of 66 come together again two miles (3km) south of the town, and the road continues towards Hamel and Edwardsville.

Left: A Route 66 souvenir probably dating from the late 1950s.

Hamel, about 13 miles (20km) from Mt. Olive, once boasted a direct street car link to St. Louis, and the electrical conductors that powered it are still visible from 66 as it passes through the town. The service was discontinued shortly before I-55 bypassed the area in the early 1960s; and as Hamel's mayor, Bill Meyer, told a reporter from the *Edwardsville Intelligencer*, "It seems like after the street car was gone and Interstate 55 was built the traffic [through the town] just disappeared." The decommissioning of 66 had a similar effect elsewhere; many of the once-busy motor lodges and other businesses lining the roads through Edwardsville and Mitchell have now been abandoned. Some of them, however — like Edwardsville's Apple Valley Motel, near I-270 (which crosses the river into St. Louis north of the historic Chain of Rocks Bridge — see pages 62-63) continue to cater for the tourists who seek out this part of the highway.

Right: Route 66 memorabilia like this remain ever popular with travelers on the Mother Road.

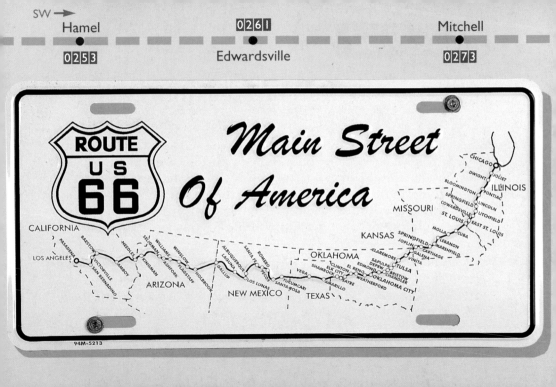

Old-Fashioned Meatloaf

MAKES 6-8 SERVINGS

Meatloaf began to appear in the US during the early 1900s. It quickly became a favorite in homes throughout the nation, and at diners and restaurants up and down Route 66 (many of which, like the Dixie Trucker's Home in McLean, Illinois, have their own special recipes for it). A simple, economical, and satisfying dish, it is as American as the apple pie with which many hungry travelers follow it!

Vegetable oil spray or vegetable oil, for greasing

1 cup rolled oats

½ cup whipping cream or half-and-half

2 tablespoons butter

1 large onion, chopped

2 garlic cloves, finely chopped

2 stalks celery, finely chopped

Continued—

Worcestershire or soy
sauce

1 pound ground pork or
bulk sausage meat

2 eggs, lightly beaten

1/2 cup chopped fresh
parsley

1 teaspoon dried thyme

1 teaspoon dried sage

1 1/2 teaspoons salt

1 teaspoon freshly
ground black pepper
or 1/2 teaspoon hot
pepper sauce

1/2 tablespoon

1/2 cup tomato sauce
plus extra for glazing

6 slices bacon, flattened
with a knife.

2 pounds ground beef

1. Preheat the oven to 350°F. Spray a large jelly roll pan with a vegetable spray or brush with oil. Put the rolled oats in a bowl and stir in the cream or half and half until combined. Set aside.

2. In a medium frying pan over medium heat, heat the butter. Add the onion and cook, stirring, for about 5 minutes, until softened and translucent. Stir in the garlic and celery and cook for 2 more minutes, stirring frequently. Set aside.

3. In a large mixing bowl with a fork or with your fingers, combine the beef and pork or sausage meat. Using a large wooden spoon or your hands, stir in the remaining ingredients, except the bacon slices, until just blended. Add the cooled onion mixture and reserved rolled oats and cream, and mix lightly to combine. Do not overwork the mixture or it will be too compact.

4. Shape the meat mixture into an oval loaf and set on the jelly roll pan. Lay the bacon strips crosswise over the loaf, tucking the ends under the edges of the loaf. Brush with a little extra tomato sauce or ketchup.

5. Bake the meat loaf for 1-1¼ hours, until well browned, glazing with the juices and drippings in the pan and brushing with a little more tomato sauce or ketchup if you like. Remove from the oven and allow to stand for about 10 minutes before slicing. You can use the drippings to make gravy.

The approach to St. Louis on 66 provides a sharp contrast with what has gone before. Bob Moore and Patrick Grauwels comment in their *Illustrated Guidebook to the Mother Road* that "Many of the older buildings, so carefully preserved in the rural locations, are being allowed to rot. [...] 50s era motels stand alongside [the highway], their glittery signs harking back to a time when this was 'The Road'." Alongside the disused diners and gas stations are old drive-in theaters such as the Bel Air, near the intersection with Illinois 111, north of Mitchell. Drive-ins, where customers watch movies from their cars, were a product of the Depression years, and retained their popularity for decades afterwards; but while a number are still in business along Route 66, the Bel Air has now closed. However, the Luna Café, shown here and situated a mile south of the theater, remains a popular place for travelers to relax before continuing their journey west.

Left: An enticing sign for the hungry motorist: the Luna Café, near Mitchell.

Mitchell
0273

0286
East St. Louis

Mississippi   River

St. Louis
0290

East St. Louis occupies the last few miles of Route 66 in Illinois. Over the years, according to a *Route 66 Magazine* article by Jim Powell, the highway has crossed the Mississippi into St. Louis via different bridges. Initially, it used the McKinley Bridge, which carried traffic from the east bank of the river to St. Louis' 9th Street. This route had probably not been the planners' original choice, but was selected after difficulties over rights of way; once these were resolved, a new stretch of road was built to link 66 with St. Louis' Municipal "Free" Bridge, which it used from about 1929.

Both these bridges led into central St. Louis; but after 1936, another alignment, via the more northerly Chain of Rocks bridge, was introduced; this had the advantage of avoiding the downtown area. The Chain of Rocks bridge, one of Missouri's proudest possessions, is profiled in more detail on the next two pages.

Right: An illustrated map c. 1960 showing some of the sights associated with 66.

The Chain of Rocks Bridge

ROUTE 66

The Chain of Rocks Bridge (namesake of the nearby natural ridge of rocks in the Mississippi River) opened in 1929 and saw its last vehicle traffic in 1968 when Interstate 270, north of the bridge, was completed. Built at a cost of $2,000,000, it is 5,353 feet (1,632m) long, 24 feet (7m) wide, and has a 22-degree angle in its span — a constant hazard for drivers. The bridge is an important icon of the highway's heritage; it has been restored, and is now open to pedestrian traffic.

Missouri

St. Louis, Missouri's largest city, is also the biggest urban center between Chicago and Los Angeles. It has been an important gateway to the West for hundreds of years; and Route 66, as it heads down towards the Ozarks, follows the path of highways and trails dating back to the Civil War or earlier. These older thoroughfares had, of course, been unpaved, but in the years following World War I, Missouri was assiduous in the upgrading of its roads. The state's first section of concreted highway was laid between Carthage and Joplin in 1920, and by the early 1930s the entire 300-mile (483km) stretch of Route 66 from St. Louis to the Kansas state line had also been given an all-weather, paved, "high-type" surface.

MISSOURI

Landscape & Climate

Missouri is often described as the state "where the forest meets the prairie." The region contains over 1.5 million acres (610,000ha) of woodland, as well as rivers, rolling hills, and networks of caves such as the famous Meramec Caverns near Stanton (see pages 80-81). Further south is the Ozark Plateau, stretching across Missouri and adjacent areas of Oklahoma and Arkansas, where the Ozark Mountains reach their highest peaks. Springfield, the "Queen City of the Ozarks" (about 225 miles [362km] from St. Louis) is an ideal starting-point for exploring these surrounding highlands. Typical temperatures for the state range from 27°F (-2°C) in January to an average of 77°F (25°C) in July.

VOICE OF THE ROAD →

We arrived in St. Louis at noon. I took a walk down by the Mississippi River and watched the logs that came floating from Montana in the north – grand Odyssean logs of our continental dream. Old steamboats with their scrollwork more scrolled and withered by weathers sat in the mud inhabited by rats. Great clouds of afternoon overtopped the Mississippi Valley.

(from On The Road *by Jack Kerouac, 1957)*

Above: Beside the Mississippi River, St. Louis, Missouri.

Below: Outside Ted Drewes Frozen Custard on Chippewa Street.

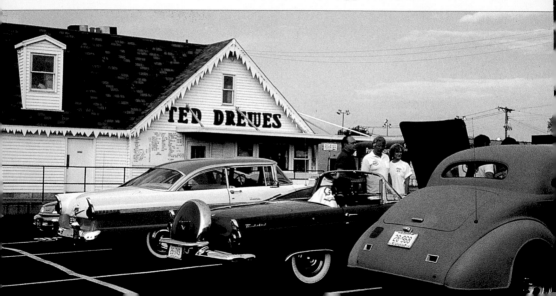

Having crossed the river, Route 66 took a number of varying paths through St. Louis during different periods. The best of these — for travelers with a sweet tooth — leads along Gravois Avenue and onto Chippewa Street, the home of Ted Drewes Frozen

Custard, makers of the city's most famous ice cream. Ted Drewes' father, Ted Sr, launched his first ice cream store in St. Louis in 1930. The following year, he established a stand on Gravois Avenue, which is still in operation. The firm's Chippewa Street premises opened in 1941, and have since been expanded and improved by Ted Jr, who took over the business after his father's death. Ted has always refused offers from franchisers eager to capitalize on his name and recipes; as he says, "It's a matter of quality. Franchising could lead to mediocrity." He does, however, provide a courier service for his ice cream, which can now be ordered via the Internet!

SW ➤ Mississippi River

0290
St. Louis ●

Eureka
● 0327

Another famous nearby landmark, the Coral Court Motel (see pages 74-75) has recently been demolished; but after turning onto Watson Road and heading about four miles (6.5km) southwest down State Highway 366, travelers can still see the "66" Park In Theatre in the suburb of Crestwood. Built in 1948, it was once a major attraction for mobile moviegoers. As well as pictures and popcorn, it offered its patrons air-conditioning ("cool breezes"), baby bottle warmers, and even a Ferris wheel. In his *Route 66 — The Mother Road*, Michael Wallis describes how, during the 1950s and 60s, "cars, trucks, campers and even school buses [would stand] bumper to bumper for blocks" as they queued to get in. Sadly, the "66" Park In is now closed to customers.

Route 66, running close to I-44, continues the journey away from St. Louis through the Sunset Hills district; it then crosses the Meramec River, heading towards the town of Eureka.

Below: Crestwood's "66" Park In Theatre, now sadly defunct.

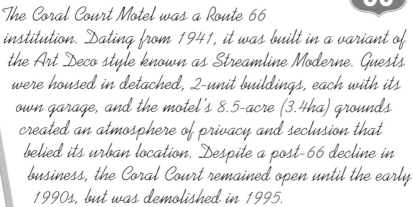

Coral Court Motel, St. Louis

The Coral Court Motel was a Route 66 institution. Dating from 1941, it was built in a variant of the Art Deco style known as Streamline Moderne. Guests were housed in detached, 2-unit buildings, each with its own garage, and the motel's 8.5-acre (3.4ha) grounds created an atmosphere of privacy and seclusion that belied its urban location. Despite a post-66 decline in business, the Coral Court remained open until the early 1990s, but was demolished in 1995.

Eureka lies just off the path of I-44 and
Route 66. Thousands of visitors a year are
attracted to the "Six Flags" theme park a
few miles away, but Eureka's most unique
claim to fame is the Black Madonna
Shrine, built near the town by a Polish
monk, Brother Bronislaus Luszcz. It was
conceived as a tribute to the original
Black Madonna, also known as Our Lady
of Czestochowa — an ancient painting of
the Virgin and Christ Child, associated
with a number of miracles, and preserved
at Czestochowa in Poland. Luszcz worked
on the Eureka shrine from 1938 until his
death in 1960; its open-air chapel has a

copy of the Black Madonna painting on its altar, and there is a complex of seven grottos with devotional statues. The shrine is decorated using shells, jewelry, and other materials donated by visitors or found by the enterprising Brother Luszcz, including cake molds and glass from old jars.

Left: One of the seven elaborately ornamented grottoes of the Black Madonna Shrine near Eureka. The site attracts pilgrims and tourists from all over the world.

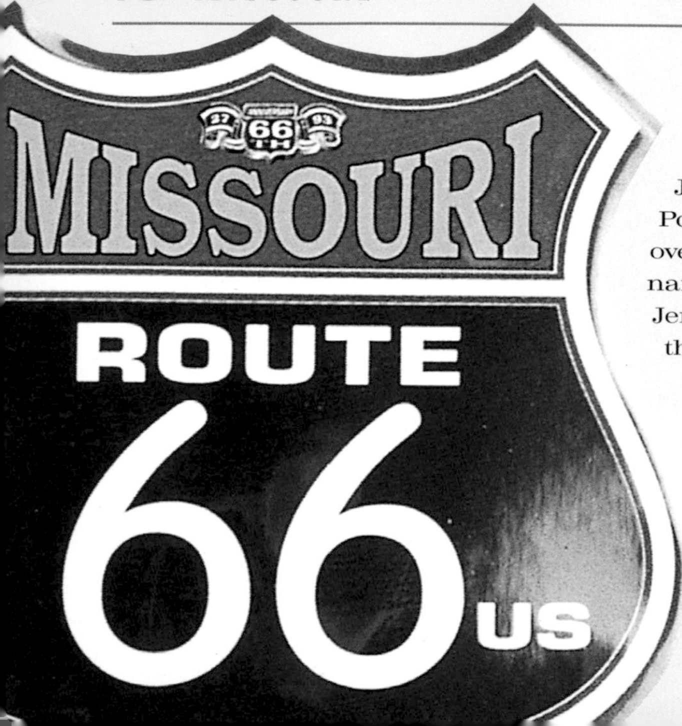

Route 66 leads from Eureka towards Pacific. Just outside it is Jensen Point, a rocky hilltop overlooking the highway, named for Lars Peter Jensen, who presided over the development of the Missouri Botanical Garden in St. Louis. The road now climbs towards Gray Summit and the entrance to the Shaw Arboretum - an extension of the

Missouri Botanical Garden opened in 1926 when airborne pollution at its main site became a potential threat to the plant collections held there. The 2,500-acre (1,012ha) Arboretum includes an Ecological Reserve, a Wildflower Garden, and a variety of other managed plant collections which can be enjoyed by visitors.

Beyond Gray Summit lie St. Clair and, nine miles (14km) further west, Stanton — the gateway to the famous Meramec Caverns, described (in the publicity signs along the roads leading to them) as the "Greatest Show Under the Earth." They are described in more detail on the next two pages.

Above: Promotional material helped to turn Route 66 into a national institution.

MERAMEC CAVERNS

Missouri boasts over 6,000 other surveyed cave sites, but the scale and grandeur of the Meramec Caverns is unsurpassed. Once a hideout for (among many others) the Jesse James Gang, the area's most famous feature is its so-called Stage Curtain: a 70-foot high, 60-foot wide, and 35-foot thick (21 x 18 x 11m) mineral deposit recognized as the largest single cave formation in the world. The Caverns are open for regular guided tours throughout the year.

Sullivan, about five miles (8km) from Stanton, was the birthplace of George Hearst (1820–1891), father of the great newspaper magnate William Randolph Hearst. George married a local schoolteacher, made his fortune as a prospector and rancher, and eventually settled in California, becoming a US Senator.

After leaving Sullivan, the road continues through Bourbon and on to Cuba, home of the Mount Pleasant Winery, whose Abbey Vineyard is open daily for tasting. Many of the grapes in this region were originally planted by Italian émigrés, who also founded the nearby town of Rosati. Fifteen miles (24km)

SW →

0358		0369		0391	
Stanton	Sullivan	Bourbon	Cuba	Rosati	Rolla
	0363		0379		0406

away is Rolla, where, in 1931, a massive St. Patrick's Day celebration was held to mark the completion of concreting on 66 in Missouri. The guests included Cyrus Avery, the "Father of the Road," and, according to Susan Croce Kelly's *Route 66*, "the whole crowd was treated to a parade of covered wagons and motor cars that stretched for two miles along the newly paved highway."

Right: The famous Mobil "Pegasus" mascot at Rolla Motors. The flying horse symbol was first used by Mobil as a corporate logo in 1931.

Rolla, a thriving community with a population approaching 15,000, and its own college campus (an offshoot of the University of Missouri, specializing in engineering and science) has always been an important staging post for travelers. Riders once watered their horses at Martin Springs, just outside the town, and the area is dotted with long-established roadside outlets offering food, accommodation, and gas. However, a stark contrast to these flourishing businesses can be seen near Arlington, just a few miles away. There, a sign and some abandoned shacks are all that remain of "John's Modern Cabins" — whose very name now has an ironic ring to it. Writing in *Route 66 Magazine*, Jerry McClanahan described John's and the other ruined motels and stores that lie alongside the highway as places where "once cash registers rang to the peal of commerce, [but] now only echoes of dim memories sigh through vacant window frames."

Left: The derelict remains of John's Modern Cabins, not far from Arlington.

The 460lb (209kg) Indian Four was a 30hp motorcycle with a 1265cc engine. At a price of $445, it appealed chiefly to the wealthier "gentleman rider."

1929 Indian Four

Indian motorcycles, manufactured in Springfield,
Massachusetts, were favorites with American riders
for more than half a century. In 1929, Indian
launched the "Four" — based on an original
design by the Ace company, which had closed
five years earlier. The reworked model was well
received, but the onset of the Depression
meant that only c.500 were built that year.

*Left: Indian's version of the Four was about 50lb
(23kg) heavier than its Ace-built predecessor.*

The road continues through Missouri, skirting the edges of the Mark Twain National Forest, which stretches alongside I-44 for more than 20 miles (32km) beyond Rolla. East of Arlington is part of the "Trail of Tears," the path taken by Native American tribes who were driven from their original homelands in Mississippi, Alabama, and Georgia in the 1830s; more than a quarter of them died on their 1,000-mile (1,600km) journey.

66 now approaches Devil's Elbow, a bend in the Big Piney River, given its name by lumberjacks who had to clear the logjams that built up there. The setting, and

Left: Gateway to a site commemorating the "Trail of Tears" through Missouri.

Above: The hazardous approach to the bridge over the Big Piney River at Devil's Elbow.

the old steel-truss road bridge, are picturesque, but this stretch of the highway, now bypassed by I-44, had a fearsome reputation for accidents. One traveler, quoted in Susan Croce Kelly's *Route 66*, describes it as "the death's corner of the world," and remembers that his father "would get white knuckles ten minutes before we'd [drive] through there."

Right: A model of an old-style gas pump of the kind once common on Route 66.

Fort Leonard Wood, the premier training facility for the US Army, is sited on the western side of the road, about five miles (8km) from the town of Waynesville. Its establishment, in 1940, had a considerable impact on the entire area; as the fort grew, it swallowed up neighboring towns such as Bloodland, Cookville, and Wharton, attracting a massive influx of construction workers in addition to the soldiers who were stationed there. Today, it occupies over 63,000 acres (25,500ha), houses the Army's Maneuver Support Center, and trains 187 National Guard units; with an annual budget of $500 million, it is by far the largest industry in Central Missouri.

The highway passes the fort as it heads west on its way towards Buckhorn and Hazelgreen — where 66 crosses the Gasconade River via a steel-truss bridge similar in design to the one at Devil's Elbow. From here, is only a short distance to the town of Lebanon.

MUSIC OF THE ROAD →

Chuck Berry, born in St. Louis in 1926, provided a rock and roll soundtrack for countless journeys down Route 66. His music was great to drive to, his lyrics reflected the lives and desires of his audience — and his first big hit, *Maybellene*, has all the ingredients of a classic road song: a boy in a V8 Ford, a girl in a Cadillac, and a strong undertow of speed and sex.

Berry recorded the song in Chicago (for the famous Chess rhythm & blues label) in 1955, and over the next few years he went on to create a string of singles that have become rock and roll anthems, including *Roll Over Beethoven*, *Sweet Little Sixteen*, and *Johnny B. Goode*. Berry was rock and roll's first great black singer/songwriter, and his music retains a huge influence and appeal for musicians and audiences across the globe.

Right: The headstock of a Gibson ES-350 electric guitar — the model favored by Chuck Berry for many of his classic recordings.

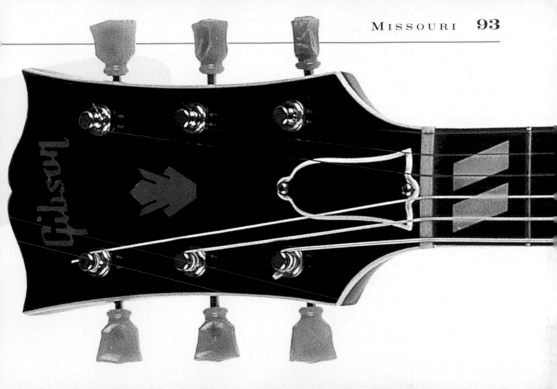

The original Munger Moss was a restaurant at Devil's Elbow; but its owners, Pete and Jessie Hudson, were forced to move when the road there was diverted away from their premises after widening work in 1945. They relocated to Lebanon, bought a café on the city's East Seminole Street, gave it the same name as their own premises, and converted it to a motel which remains one of the most distinctive landmarks on Route 66.

Munger Moss Motel
"on old Rt. 66" Lebanon, Missouri.- Built in 1946

-1946-

Like most lodging-places on America's highways, the Munger Moss has moved with the times. In the late 1940s, it housed its guests in individual cabins; but

Above: An early postcard of the Munger Moss Motel.

these separate units were later joined together, creating a modern-style motel. Longer-established businesses were also evolving rapidly. Lebanon's Camp Joy, situated nearby, started out in the 1920s as an auto camp, providing its patrons with little more than tents and parking places; however, it too was soon offering the more comprehensive and comfortable facilities demanded by post-war travelers.

Left: How the Munger Moss Motel announces itself to passers-by today.

The 50-mile (80km) journey from Lebanon to Springfield, the "Queen City of the Ozarks," leads through the towns of Phillipsburg and Conway — both part of Laclede County, for which Lebanon is the county seat. The highway and railroad run parallel with each other for long distances, and near some sections of 66 is an even older path: the so-called Wire Road, a rocky surface holding the telegraph poles that carried military communications between Jefferson Barracks in St. Louis and Fort Smith, Arkansas. This 400-mile (644km) link, begun in 1859 and completed a few years later, was one of the longest lines of communication in America prior to the introduction of the first transcontinental telegraph in 1861. The Wire Road came into its own during the Civil War, not only for sending messages, but also as a reliable pathway for soldiers to march on; an active campaign is currently under way to preserve it.

Right: A sign for one of the many franchises offering drive-in food "to go" on Route 66 in Missouri.

VOICE OF THE ROAD →

66 Talk about a rule of iron – we had it. 99

("Wild Bill" Hickok, who shot gunfighter Dave Tutt in Springfield, Missouri, 1865)

Springfield has a fascinating and turbulent history, and there are many excellent opportunities for visitors to discover its past for themselves. The Battle of Wilson's Creek in 1861, during which more than 2,500 Union and Confederate soldiers lost their lives, took place just south of the city; the site of the conflict is now a designated National Battlefield, with a Visitor Center providing information, exhibits, and maps. Springfield is also famous for its links with "Wild Bill" Hickok (1837—76). The famous frontiersman had a shoot-out with a gunfighter named Dave Tutt in the city one

Above: The Battle of Wilson's Creek, which took place just south of Springfield in 1861.

Sunday morning in 1865, following an argument over the loss of Hickok's watch in a poker game the night before. Both men drew their weapons at the same time, but Hickok shot first, killing Tutt before he could return fire. Wild Bill was later tried for Tutt's murder, but acquitted after the prosecution failed to prove that he had been the aggressor.

Above: A "Route 66" souvenir wall lamp bearing the Mother Road's famous shield.

Springfield

0515

Today, Springfield offers a wide range of attractions to visitors. In the city itself is the Landers Theater, the longest-established playhouse in Missouri, built in 1909 and recently restored to its original glory. Famous names such as John Philip Sousa (the "March King") and Lillian Russell once appeared there, and since the Landers was taken over by the Springfield Little Theater organization in 1970, it has become a major center for plays, concerts, and ballets. It also provided early encouragement for many current stars, notably Kathleen Turner, who was born in Springfield.

The surrounding area features wineries, hiking trails, and a scenic railway; and five miles (8km) outside the city is the Crystal Cave, a natural cavern first opened to the public in 1893, after electric lighting had been installed there. The cave is temperature-controlled, and provides a comfortable and safe environment in which to examine spectacular rock formations and waterfalls.

Right: A welcome sight for the weary traveler — food and cold beer aplenty.

Pork 'n' Herb Sausage Patties

MAKES 12 PATTIES

Away from the freeways and the predictability of their fast food franchises, travelers on Route 66 are much more likely to encounter some of the old-style roadhouse cafés offering a genuine taste of the region's cuisine. Sausage patties like these were once a staple of such places — but are now harder to track down.

1 1/2 pounds lean ground pork

1/3 cup fresh white bread crumbs

1 large egg, lightly beaten

2 tablespoons freshly chopped parsley

2 teaspoons chopped fresh sage leaves or 1 teaspoon dried sage

1/2 teaspoon hot pepper sauce

2 green onions (scallions), finely chopped

CONTINUED —

Route Food

Salt and freshly
ground black
pepper

Bacon drippings or
vegetable oil, for
frying

1/2 teaspoon ground
allspice

1. Put the ground pork in a large mixing bowl and add all the remaining ingredients except the bacon drippings or oil. Using a fork or your fingers, gently mix until just combined.

2. Working with wet hands, shape the mixture into twelve 2½-inch patties. Arrange on a baking sheet and refrigerate, covered, for at least 30 minutes or overnight.

3. In a large, heavy-bottomed skillet or griddle, heat 2 tablespoons of bacon drippings or oil over medium heat. Add the patties to the pan and cook for about 10 minutes, until the meat is cooked through and the patties are crisp and brown, turning at least once.

Right: A late 1950s Cadillac Eldorado
Seville — the driver's refueling!

Do not overcrowd — if necessary, cook in 2 batches and keep warm in a medium oven. Drain on paper towels and serve hot with fried cornmeal mush or scrambled or fried eggs.

W →

Springfield

0533

Phelps

0570

0515

Halltown

0548

Carthage

Beyond Springfield, State Highway 96 follows the original path of Route 66 via Halltown and Phelps to Carthage — the site of a Civil War victory over the Union forces by the Missouri State Guard in 1861, and later a focus for action by Southern fighters. Among them was Myra Maybelle Shirley — better known as Belle Starr — who was a courier for the Quantrill Missouri Guerrillas during the conflict. Belle, a native of Carthage, subsequently became involved in horse stealing, and was already notorious as a "Bandit Queen" before her marriage to Sam Starr in 1880. She was shot by an unknown assailant in Oklahoma nine years later.

Belle Starr and other famous residents of Carthage are commemorated close to its central courthouse, with a mural by distinguished local artist Lowell Davis illustrating scenes from the town's history. Carthage's many other attractions include the nearby 66 Drive-In Theatre — one of the few still operating along the highway.

Left: Open for business — the 66 Drive-In Theatre just outside Carthage, Missouri.

The 15-mile (24km) stretch of Route 66 from Carthage to Joplin was the first section of paved road to be laid in Missouri. Originally named Route 14, and built to accommodate the heavy traffic created by zinc and lead mining in the area, it was incorporated into 66 after 1926. The mines are now gone, but the area (which proudly describes itself as "The Gateway to the Ozarks") still attracts plenty of travelers. One of its most striking landmarks is the "Praying Hands" sculpture mounted on a grassy mound near Webb City, and

Left: Webb City's "Praying Hands," flanked by the Stars and Stripes.

flanked by two American
flags. Designed by Jack
Dawson and erected in 1973,
its pedestal bears the
inscription "Hands in Prayer
— World in Peace." Joplin lies
five miles (8km) further west,
and after passing down its
Main Street, 66 completes its
last few miles in Missouri,
continuing across the State
line into Kansas.

*Left: In Missouri corn, wheat, and
cotton are the staple crops.*

The Mustang was available with a variety of engine options. Initially, the most powerful of these was a 4.7 liter V8 that could deliver a top speed of 118mph (190kph). By 1967, Ford was offering the car with a 6.4 liter engine capable of 125mph (201kph).

1965 Ford Mustang GT Coupe

Youth and fast cars go together – and Ford, who had previously lacked a sporting profile, created the Mustang as a racy, "total performance" car for the affluent young drivers of the 1960s. Launched in 1964, and available as a hardtop coupé or a convertible, the Mustang's sleek design and impressive performance gave Ford's target market exactly what it wanted. By 1966, over a million Mustangs had been produced.

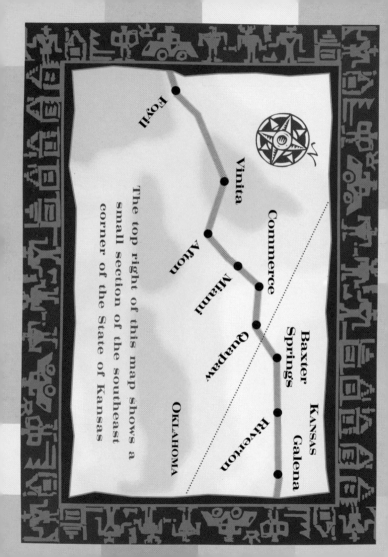

Foyil

Vinita

Commerce

Afton

Miami

Quapaw

Baxter Springs

KANSAS
Galena

Riverton

OKLAHOMA

The top right of this map shows a small section of the southeast corner of the State of Kansas

Kansas

Only 15 miles (24km) of Route 66 are in Kansas; the road passes across its southeastern corner, taking in Galena, Riverton, and Baxter Springs before crossing into Oklahoma. Kansas, the former trailhead for two great pioneering routes, the Santa Fe and Oregon Trails, might have been expected to disdain such a tiny section of highway. But instead, as Michael Wallis points out in his study of *Route 66: The Mother Road*, "[it] was a source of pride to the rugged miners, farmers and small town merchants. It brought the rest of the nation through their territory." And although 66's journey through Kansas is short, it provides us with a vivid insight into the fascinating history of the "Sunflower State."

The introduction of the Will Rogers Turnpike in 1953 made it possible to drive directly from Joplin, Missouri to Tulsa, Oklahoma without passing through Kansas at all. But the older road we explore here retains its interest and charm, and even its signposting has a distinctive look. Kansas has its own special Route 66 marker — a black "66" on a yellow sunflower; and the state also helps visitors stay on track by painting the standard "66" shield directly onto the pavement in some places.

However, compared to the variety of alignments found on parts of Illinois and Missouri, the path taken by the highway through Kansas is relatively uncomplicated. At the border with Missouri, there is a choice between continuing in a straight line along SR66, or making a right-hand turn and following an earlier stretch of road. Selecting the path of "Old Route 66" here quickly leads the traveler towards the town of Galena.

Left: Agriculture flourishes on Kansas' rich farmlands.
Grain and cattle are especially important.

The launch of Route 66 coincided with Kansas City's emergence as a major regional center for popular music — which was due, in part, to the civic authorities' relaxed attitude towards club licensing and alcohol (even during Prohibition). In his autobiography, *Good Morning Blues,* pianist and bandleader Count Basie describes K.C. as "a musicians' town, [where] there were good musicians everywhere you turned." One of his regular gigs was at a venue near a hospital where "sometimes, when things were really jumping...there would be [patients] leaning out of the windows, playing their horns. I'd never seen or heard anything like that in my life." Basie assembled the nucleus of his own famous orchestra in the city during the mid-1930s; and its growing fame was given a substantial boost by regular radio broadcasts on station W9XBY, which relayed the band's distinctive sound throughout the state of Kansas, and as far afield as Minneapolis and Chicago.

Left: Kansas City was the birthplace of the great bebop saxophonist Charlie Parker.

Galena

0590

Galena, like many other places in the Tri-State region where Kansas, Missouri, and Oklahoma meet, was once an important center for lead and zinc mining; the company that ran these operations, Eagle-Picher, still retains a plant in town, although the mines themselves are now exhausted.

Mineral extraction brought prosperity to Galena, but during the 1930s there was severe labor unrest within the industry. In 1935, attacks by unionized workers on strike breakers led to the temporary blockage of Route 66 in the area,

Right: A gas station in Galena — one of the few on the Kansas stretch of Route 66.

and two years later, a shooting incident outside a union headquarters in the town claimed the lives of nine men. These events, and other aspects of Galena's past, can be studied in its Mining and Historical Museum, sited in a former railroad depot, and run for many years by Howard Litch, a miner's son, ex-Galena garage proprietor, and longtime resident of the town. Mr. Litch died in 1996, at the age of 90.

Above: Texas oil attracted the railroad to head south through Kansas.

In 1929, racer Arthur Fournier rode a stripped version of the Tornado to a speed of 108mph (174kph) at Playa Del Rey, California. This was the final year of production.

1929 Cleveland Tornado

The 1929 Cleveland Tornado, with its top speed of 100mph (161kph), would have made fast work of Route 66's well-paved Kansas section. At 1000cc, it was the most powerful model ever produced by the Ohio-based firm, whose earlier motorcycles had often been outperformed by bigger-engined rivals. Sadly, only a few months after the Tornado's appearance, Cleveland was wiped out in the aftermath of the Wall Street Crash.

Left: The Tornado's gas tank reflected the trend for streamlining.

SW →

0590

Riverton

0603

Galena

0596

Baxter Springs

Before entering Riverton, the road originally crossed the Spring River via a Marsh Rainbow Arch Bridge, dating from the 1920s; sadly, this was demolished in 1986. More recently, Riverton lost another of its best known landmarks: the Spring River Inn, built in 1902, and famous for its superb cuisine, served in a dining room overlooking the water. The restaurant closed in 1996, and was destroyed by fire two years later. Thankfully, the town's Eisler Brothers General Store, run by Scott Nelson, President of the Kansas Historic Route 66 Association, continues to thrive, selling an excellent selection of memorabilia alongside the groceries and ice cream.

At Riverton US66 becomes US69, and turns south a little way beyond the river. However, to see one of the highlights of Old Route 66 in Kansas, a surviving Marsh Rainbow Arch Bridge, travelers should continue west, following an earlier alignment of the road.

Below: Eisler Bros. store in Riverton doubles as the HQ of Kansas' Historic Route 66 Association.

RAINBOW ARCH BRIDGE

ROUTE 66

The "Rainbow" or "Marsh Arch"-style road bridge, created by engineer James Barney Marsh (1854–1936), was an elegant design whose surviving examples are being carefully preserved. This one, built in 1923, crosses Brush Creek just less than four miles (6.4km) north of Baxter Springs, on an early alignment of Route 66. Known as the "Graffiti Bridge" (due to the inscriptions left on it by "road pilgrims"), it has recently been restored by the Kansas Historic Route 66 Association.

SW ➝

Riverton

0603

OKLAHOMA

0596

Baxter Springs

A few miles beyond the Rainbow Arch Bridge, the road enters Baxter Springs, once a key staging post for cattle being driven from Texas on the Shawnee Trail. In 1863, during the Civil War, it was the site of the Baxter Springs Massacre, in which Lt. Col. William C. Quantrill (organizer of the Quantrill Missouri Guerrillas — see pages 108-9) captured and killed almost an entire detachment of Union forces. Men from both sides who died in the fighting are commemorated in the town's cemetery.

Baxter Springs is also alleged to have been the target of a bank raid by Jesse James in 1876; while there is little firm evidence for this story, another bandit, Henry Starr, is known to have robbed a downtown bank in 1914. The building he attacked is now the site of Bill Murphey's Restaurant — a good place to enjoy a final meal in Kansas before traveling the short distance to the Oklahoma border.

Right: Cattle pens in Kansas — livestock has been a key factor in the area's economy for over 150 years.

Deluxe Grilled Cheese & Bacon Sandwiches

MAKES 4 SANDWICHES

Sandwiches were always available on 66, although they were rarely as delicious as this one, made with Gruyère or Monterey Jack, not the process cheese that was a staple in many roadside snack bars.

8 tablespoons (1 stick) butter, softened

2 tablespoons Dijon-style mustard

1 tablespoon finely minced thyme leaves

1 tablespoon freshly chopped parsley

Freshly ground black pepper

1/2 pound bacon (at least 12 slices), cooked until crisp and drained

8 slices firm white bread

1/2 pound cheddar, Gruyère, or Monterey

Jack cheese, thinly sliced

1-2 large tomatoes, thinly sliced

1 small red onion, thinly sliced

Vegetable oil spray or vegetable oil

Route Food

1. In a small bowl with a wooden spoon, cream the butter, mustard, thyme, and parsley until well blended. Season with freshly ground black pepper.

2. Arrange the slices of bread on a work surface and spread very lightly with half the butter mixture. Divide half the cheese between 4 of the bread slices. Top each with 4 slices of crispy bacon — trim to fit if necessary. Cover each with tomato and onion slices, then top each with the remaining cheese slices and cover with the remaining 4 bread slices. Spread the remaining herb butter on the outside of the sandwich tops and bottoms.

3. Spray a large nonstick skillet or griddle with a vegetable oil cooking spray or brush lightly with oil. Set over medium heat until hot. Add the sandwiches (work in batches if necessary), and cook for about 3 minutes, until the bottoms are golden and crisp. Carefully turn the

Right: Cattlemen have hearty appetites — so do travelers on 66!

sandwiches and cook for about 3 minutes more, until golden and the cheese is just melted. Remove to a work surface, cut in half, and serve immediately.

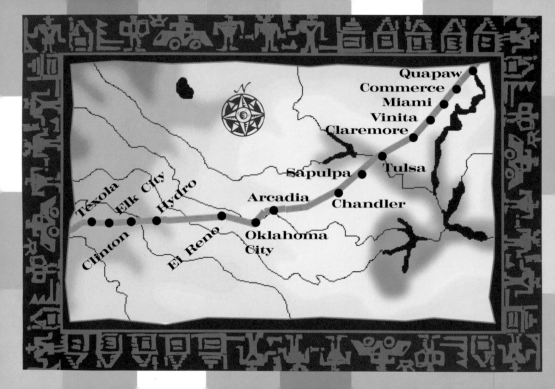

Oklahoma

Rodgers and Hammerstein's classic musical *Oklahoma!* concludes with its hero and heroine, Curly and Laurey, looking forward to "living in a brand new state." The show was set in the early 1900s, when Oklahoma had existed as a Territory for little more than a decade; many of its pioneering inhabitants had acquired their lands by lottery, or simply by staking a claim. Oklahoma achieved statehood in 1907, and Route 66's path through it, from the Kansas border to Texola, almost 380 miles (612km) further west, takes in many of the places immortalized by John Steinbeck, Woody Guthrie, and the other artists who have charted its struggles and triumphs over the past century.

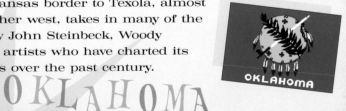

OKLAHOMA

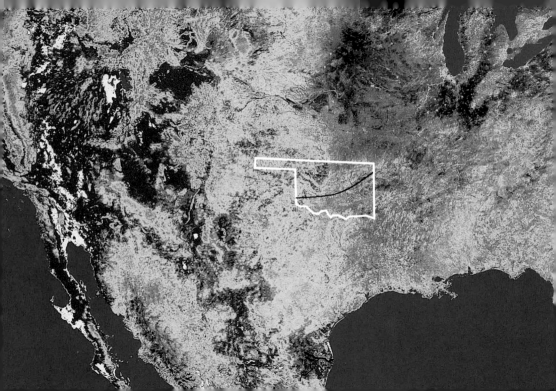

Landscape & Climate

Route 66 enters Oklahoma at its northeastern corner, where the "green country" surrounding the road to Tulsa closely resembles the nearby terrain of southern Missouri. Further southwest, prairie land predominates, and some regions are prone to tornadoes: one especially severe "twister" caused extensive devastation south and east of Oklahoma City (an area known as "Tornado Alley") in May 1999, and rebuilding is likely to take two to three years. Oklahoma is sometimes described as the land of "soil, oil, and toil," and although its farmers and oil workers have faced recent economic hardships, these are being overcome with the same resilience that saw the state through the Dustbowl years of the 1930s.

66 is the path of a people in flight, refugees from dust and shrinking land, from the thunder of tractors and shrinking ownership, from the desert's slow northward invasion, from the twisting winds that howl up out of Texas, from the floods that bring no richness to the land and steal what little richness is there. From all of these the people are in flight, and they come into 66 from the tributary side roads, from the wagon tracks and the rutted country roads. 66 is the mother road, the road of flight.

(from The Grapes of Wrath *by John Steinbeck, 1939)*

Right: Escaping the Dust Bowl — one of a famous series of 1930s photos by Dorothea Lange.

THE GRAPES OF WRATH

The region around Quapaw, about four miles (6.5km) from the Kansas/Oklahoma state line, is another former lead- and zinc-mining area, with mounds of leftover waste from the excavations still lying by the roadside. Nearby is Commerce, where Micky Mantle, one of America's greatest baseball players, grew up in the 1930s and 1940s. Mantle, whose father was a miner, replaced Joe DiMaggio as center field for the New York Yankees, and Commerce's Micky Mantle Boulevard is named in his honor.

Left: The cracked surface of the Mother Road near Quapaw.

SW →
KANSAS

0609
●
Quapaw

Commerce
●
0615

0620
●
Miami

*Above: A mural of an old gas station
on the wall of a tire shop in Quapaw.*

Miami, the next town on the
road west, boasts one of the
most striking buildings in this
part of Oklahoma: the Spanish
Colonial revival-style Coleman
Theater, built in 1929 for George
L. Coleman Sr, a local mining
magnate, and recently restored
to its original glory. Its
architects, the Boller brothers,
were also responsible for the
KiMo Theater in Albuquerque
(see pages 262-263), and both
houses remain in regular use
for movies and live events.

SW ➞

| 0620 | Afton | | 0644 | Foyil |
| Miami | 0629 | | Vinita | 0670 |

After leaving Miami, Route 66 continues towards Afton. The town, founded in 1886, was given its name, shared with the river immortalized in Robert Burns' poem *Afton Water,* by a Scottish railroad surveyor. To the north is the site of Buffalo Ranch, once a popular attraction where bison, deer, and more exotic livestock were on display to visitors — sadly, it has now closed.

On the Interstate near Vinita is "The World's Largest McDonald's". Straddling the Will Rogers Turnpike, and part of the Howard Johnson empire before being acquired by the hamburger chain, it was the first restaurant ever constructed across a public highway in America. Further west lies Foyil, hometown of Andy Payne, winner of the famous "Bunion Derby" — a transcontinental foot race run along the newly-commissioned highway in 1928. A road marker commemorates the contest, and in 1998 a statue of Payne was unveiled just south of 66 in Foyil.

Right: Afton's Buffalo Ranch, closed after more than 40 years as a Route 66 attraction.

Will Rogers Hotel, Claremore

ROUTE 66

Claremore, ten miles (16km) west of Foyil, has close links with Will Rogers (1879–1935), who started out as a rodeo performer and became a movie star, broadcaster, and newspaper columnist. The impressive downtown hotel bearing his name was launched in 1930; it attracted a string of eminent guests throughout the following decades, but went out of business in 1991. Its elegant lobby (which features a large bronze statue of Rogers) still survives, but the building has recently been converted into retirement apartments.

In 1911, Will Rogers purchased 20 acres (8ha) of hilltop land outside Claremore as a future retirement home; but his death in 1935, in a plane crash in Alaska, robbed him of the chance to enjoy it. His widow, Betty, decided that the site should become a permanent memorial to him, and accordingly, a museum and gardens were established there, open free to the public seven days a week. The museum features a wide range of

Right: The Will Rogers Memorial near Claremore.

SW →

Vinita

0670

Claremore

0644

Foyil

0680

Rogers-related material, from photographs, movie clips, and recordings of Will's radio broadcasts to riding saddles and other cowboy items. A statue of him, bearing his famous words "I never met a man I didn't like" on its base, is also displayed there, and he, his wife, and their infant son have their graves in the surrounding grounds.

Another important event commemorating this much-loved Oklahoman, the Will Rogers Memorial Rodeo, takes place every summer in nearby Vinita (see pages 142-143).

Left: The site features museums, galleries, and many other attractions.

Below: Catoosa's famous Blue Whale has recently been "made over."

SW →

Claremore
●
0680

0691
●
Catoosa

Tulsa
●
0697

After leaving Claremore, Route 66 crosses the Verdigris River and heads for the town of Catoosa, about 11 miles (18km) away. This is the home of the famous Blue Whale — a giant model cetacean with a slide in its side, once popular with swimmers using the pond where it lies. After several years' neglect, the Whale has recently been renovated, as Marian Clark reports in a recent edition of *Route 66 Magazine*. Sadly, though, a longer established Catoosa landmark, the Chief Wolf Robe Trading Post (named for an Acoma Indian renowned for his artistic skills) is now a used car lot. A few miles to the north lies the Port of Catoosa, a major inland seaport on the Arkansas River Navigation System; but Route 66 avoids the area, continuing west towards Tulsa, once known as the "Oil Capital of the World," and still one of the state's most important cities.

Cadillac sold few cars during the Depression; its parent company, General Motors, was kept afloat by cheaper marques.

1932 Cadillac V16

The introduction of Cadillac's V16 engine in 1930 was an important technical breakthrough: the company's publicity department heralded the 425 cubic inch (7 liter) design as "wholly new and express[ing] fully the contemporary conception of brilliant performance." This V16 features coachwork by the Fleetwood Body Corporation. A wide range of finishes was available, allowing the customer to "[blend] the [selection] of panels, upholstery, fabrics, trim and other factors of style and beauty... into distinctive expressions of individuality."

Tulsa was officially established in 1878; its name comes from the Tallassee or Tulsey Indian tribes who settled nearby. An oil strike in Red Fork (just across the Arkansas River) in 1901 led to a rapid growth in the town's size and prosperity, and it soon became an influential, forward-looking urban center. One of its leading officials was Cyrus Avery, who became Oklahoma's State Highway Commissioner in 1923, and was the prime mover in the planning and construction of Route 66.

Above: The outskirts of Tulsa, and the road and railtracks leading into the city.

Tulsa's oil is long gone, and while it remains a flourishing city (the second largest in the state), some of the areas Route 66 passes through are not as impressive as they once were, with the demolition of buildings like the Will Rogers Theatre and Will Rogers Motor Court on 11th Street. However, there is no shortage of eye-catching architecture in other parts of town, as we shall see on the next two pages.

Right: A model of Tulsa's Will Rogers Motor Court, now demolished.

Bob Moore and Patrick Grauwels, in their *Illustrated Guide to the Mother Road,* describe Tulsa as "an Art Deco lover's dream come true." Its notable buildings in this style include the Tulsa Monument Company on 11th Street, the imposing Fire Alarm Building on 8th, and a considerable number of stores and private houses designed by architects such as Robert M. McFarlin, Waite Phillips, and W.G. Skelly.

Tulsa also has some more recent, large-scale architecture and art. In 1965, evangelist Oral Roberts (b.1918) opened his own university in the city; the campus, on South Lewis Avenue, features 22 major buildings valued at more than $250 million, including a

Right: The Prayer Tower at Oral Roberts University includes an observation deck.

200-foot (61m) Prayer Tower completed in 1967. Roberts was also responsible for the 40-foot (12m) tall bronze "Healing Hands" sculpture that once stood in front of his City of Faith Health-Care Center. The hospital closed in 1989, and the Hands can now be seen at the entrance to Oral Roberts University.

Above: "Healing Hands" sculpture, also commissioned by Oral Roberts. The bronze hands seem to rise from the ground in prayer.

Oklahoma's most celebrated musical son, Woody Guthrie, was born in the small town of Okemah in 1912. Many of his songs convey the hardships of the Dust Bowl, and the plight of the migrant workers who, as he put it in his *Pastures of Plenty*, "come with the dust and...go with the wind" as they seek jobs and shelter. Woody's own travels began early: according to his autobiography, *Bound For Glory*, "I was a little past sixteen when I first hit the highway." In 1937, he settled in Los Angeles, achieving considerable fame as a performer and political activist; but his definitive recordings of numbers such as *This Land Is Your Land* and *Do Re Mi* were made after he moved to New York in 1940. By 1954, when his career was cut short by the onset of Huntington's chorea, he had composed over 1,000 songs. Woody Guthrie died, after many years of illness, in 1967.

Left: Poster for the 1976 movie based on Woody Guthrie's autobiography Bound For Glory, *autographed by its star, David Carradine.*

SW →

0691
Catoosa

Tulsa
0697

0712
Sapulpa

The territory now occupied by Sapulpa, about 15 miles (24km) west of Tulsa, passed through the hands of no less than five different rulers (Spain, France, Britain, Mexico, and the Choctaw Indian Nation) in the last few hundred years, before becoming part of the USA. Its first settler was a Creek Indian, Chief Sapulpa, who arrived in the area during the 1850s; in 1886, the Atlantic and Pacific Railroad built a station nearby, and the town was formally incorporated in 1898. In the wake of an oil strike six miles (10km) away at Glenpool in 1905, Sapulpa became a boom town. Today, it retains a substantial industrial base, but is perhaps best known for its Frankoma Pottery factory, established in the 1930s by the late John Frank, and now sited a mile outside the town. Sapulpa's City Hall has a mural made from Frankoma tiles, and a National Frankoma Festival is held in the town each September.

Left: No sale...Disused gas pump in a
Route 66 service station forecourt.

The 85-mile (137km) stretch of highway from Sapulpa to Arcadia leads through what one Route 66 authority, Jack Rittenhouse, described in 1946 as "rolling countryside — once the haunt of Indians, later the territory of cowmen and 'badmen,' but now principally devoted to oil and agriculture." The oil has gone, but the farmlands remain, and occasionally there are reminders of the old, lawless days. Beyond the town of Bristow lies Lincoln County, whose former sheriff, Bill Tilghman, once a deputy in Dodge City, was the man who brought Bill Doolin (leader of the infamous Wild Bunch) to justice in 1896. Tilghman himself was killed in a shootout in 1924, and is buried in the city cemetery at Chandler.

After passing through Wellston, 14 miles (23km) west of Chandler, the road continues via Luther towards Arcadia — founded as a settlement on the banks of the Deep Fork River in 1889, and famous for its distinctive Round Barn, built nine years later.

Left: Oklahoma skies — a solitary windmill dominates the landscape.

The Round Barn, Arcadia

ROUTE 66

William Harrison Odor, a local farmer and storeowner, was responsible for the building of Arcadia's Round Barn in 1898. Constructed from oak, its two stories were designed to shelter animals and store hay and grain; but from very early in its existence, the barn was also used for social events. Since its restoration by Arcadia's Historical and Preservation Society in 1992, it has become a popular venue for dances, meetings, and even weddings!

More than a million inhabitants now occupy Oklahoma City. It came into being in the wake of the great Land Rush of 1889, when President Benjamin Harrison opened up Oklahoma Territory's hitherto "Unassigned Lands" to would-be settlers. Oklahoma City (originally known as Oklahoma Station) soon became the administrative center for the surrounding area; and in 1910, when its population had grown to 64,000, a successful campaign was launched to make it the capital of the "brand new state" of Oklahoma. A massive oil strike in 1928 gave the city's fortunes an even bigger boost, and it has remained a major focus for commerce ever since.

In his *Route 66 – The Mother Road*, Michael Wallis describes "OKC" as "a pawed-over oil-field floozy...with a touch of elegance." Not everything about it is beautiful, but it combines dynamic modernity with a powerful sense of its past – as we shall see in the next two pages.

Below: A forest of flagpoles in downtown Oklahoma City.

For Oklahoma City, it all began with "The Pioneers of 1889" — and the town's frontier heritage is celebrated in a striking statue of its early settlers, which is displayed on Couch Drive.

A more detailed account of the history of the Old West can be found at the National Cowboy Hall of Fame on Persimmon Hill (NE 63rd Street). This provides a wide range of displays, portraits, and memorabilia associated with all 17 Western states. There are

Right: 66 Bowl on Oklahoma City's 39th Street Expressway.

Oklahoma City

recreations of Indian and pioneer villages, and several memorial busts and statues, including one of Buffalo Bill (William Frederick Cody), whose real-life exploits as a warrior, pioneer, and showman are now woven into the fabric of "Wild West" legend.

Other important aspects of Oklahoma City's heritage are featured at venues such as its Red Earth Indian Center, Harn Homestead Museum, and Oklahoma Heritage Center.

Above: Buffalo Bill silhouetted against the skyline at OKC's National Cowboy Hall of Fame.

The Knucklehead sold for $380, and about 1,500 were made in its first year. With its muscular engine and streamlined profile, it was widely regarded as the best-looking bike on the road.

1936 Harley-Davidson
EL Knucklehead

Harley-Davidson had planned to introduce a
1000cc, overhead-valve-engined motorcycle in
1935; however, development was slowed by the
Depression, and the model did not
appear until the following year.
Despite this delay, the stylish
new EL (nicknamed
Knucklehead because of its
bulging rocker boxes) was
an instant success — and
in the improving economic
climate, there was a growing
market for it.

Right: Top speed was 95mph (153kph).

Below: An old flourmill in Yukon. This part of Oklahoma was once a major wheat-growing area, but now much has been built over.

OKLAHOMA

YUKON'S BEST FLOUR

NO FINER OR MORE MODERN MILLS IN AMERICA

YUKON MILL & GRAIN CO.   OKLA.

W →

Oklahoma City   0831   El Reno   0889

0817   Yukon   0844   Hydro

Leaving Oklahoma City, travelers can either head west on I-40, or see as much of the Old Road as possible by using SR66. Both highways pass through Yukon, boyhood home of country music star Garth Brooks, who was born in Tulsa, and continue towards El Reno — where movie buffs may recognize the Big 8 Motel which featured in Dustin Hoffman's *Rain Man* (although its location was "moved" to Amarillo for the film). Recently, the Big 8 sign disappeared when the motel changed its name to the Deluxe Inn; it was later salvaged from a scrap dealer, and is now owned by a private collector.

No journey on Route 66 would be complete without a visit to Lucille's Service Station in Hydro, about 45 miles (72km) west of El Reno. This historic store was run by Lucille Hamons from 1941 until the 1990s; her book, *Mother of the Mother Road*, provides a fascinating glimpse of the highway's glory days.

Hydro
●
0889

0911
●
Clinton

The next major town on 66, Clinton, lies about 22 miles (35km) west of Hydro. Among its many attractions is the new Route 66 Museum on Gary Boulevard, with an impressive range of displays and memorabilia. Launched in 1995 with the aid of federal and state funds, as well as donations from Clinton residents, it houses a unique collection of vintage vehicles, a recreation of a

drive-in movie theater and Phillips service station, and a wealth of other exhibits reflecting every decade of the road's existence.

After visiting the museum, travelers in need of sustenance frequently sought out the most famous restaurant in Clinton:

Above: Clinton's new Route 66 Museum is dedicated to the preservation of vehicles, artifacts, and documents.

Pop Hick's at 223 Gary Boulevard, established in 1936, and most recently run by Howard and Mary Nichols. Pop Hick's offered round the clock service and a menu featuring traditional, satisfying food — including perennial favorites such as Shack Chicken Wings, steakburgers, and Funk's Grove Peach Cobbler. Sadly, it was destroyed by fire in August 1999.

Left: Pop Hick's in Clinton served travelers for more than 60 years.

Red-Hot BBQ
Beef Ribs

MAKES 4 SERVINGS

Among the staples on Pop Hick's menu are charcoal-grilled specialties like "Border Town Bar-B-Q Backribs" and burgers "basted with Cattleman's Bar-B-Q Sauce," which seem to carry faint echoes of the long-gone days of cowboys and chuck wagons. Back then, there was rarely time for barbecuing, which required more attention than the average trail cook could afford — but now that kitchen ranges have replaced camp fires, delicious dishes like this pose fewer difficulties.

Route Food

INGREDIENTS

*4 meaty beef ribs, 10–12 inches long and
  weighing about 1 pound each*

Vegetable oil for grilling or broiling.

SIZZLING BARBECUE SAUCE

2 tablespoons vegetable oil or beef drippings

1 large onion, very finely chopped

2 cloves garlic, very finely chopped

1 1/2 cups bottled tomato ketchup

1/2 cup bottled chilli sauce

4 tablespoons dark brown sugar

4 tablespoons lemon juice

1 tablespoon Worcestershire sauce

1/2 tablespoon hot pepper sauce, or to taste

Salt and freshly ground black pepper, to taste

1. To prepare the sauce, heat the oil in a saucepan over medium heat. Add the onion and garlic and cook, stirring occasionally, for 5-7 minutes, until softened. Stir in the remaining ingredients, lower the heat, and simmer, stirring frequently, for about 45 minutes, until the flavors blend and the sauce is slightly thickened. Taste and adjust the seasoning, if necessary.

2. Put the ribs in a non-metallic bowl large enough to hold them in a single layer. Pour the sauce over and make sure the ribs are well coated. Cover and refrigerate for at least 2 hours or overnight.

3. Prepare an outside charcoal, gas, or electric grill, or preheat a broiler. Arrange the ribs on an oiled rack, or a greased foil-lined broiler pan. cook for about 20 minutes for medium, turning the ribs regularly and basting with remaining sauce. Serve hot or at room temperature with freshly cooked corn-on-the-cob.

*Left: A stop sign in Oklahoma City
— maybe it's time to eat?*

SW →

| Clinton | 0925 | Canute | 0941 | Sayre | 0972 | Texola |
| 0911 | Foss | 0937 | Elk City | 0957 | Erick | 0979 |

Oklahoma has almost 400 miles (640km) of Route 66 — but as we journey from Clinton through Foss and Canute to Elk City, we approach the final stretch of Mother Road in this state. Elk City, originally named Busch (after Adolphus Busch, founder of the Busch-Anheuser brewery, creators of Michelob and Budweiser) is one of many communities whose livelihood was damaged when the introduction of I-40 cut them off from the main highway. Queenan's Indian Trading Post, a once-thriving retail business on the old road, closed several years ago; its ex-proprietor, Wanda Queenan, has become curator of Elk City's National Route 66 Museum. Wanda's Kachina doll, "Myrtle", which previously "stood guard" outside the Trading Post, has moved with her, and is now on display there.

Next, 66 passes through Sayre, whose attractions include a 100-year-old hotel converted into a bed-and-breakfast by proprietors Chris and Bill Lakey, and the RS&KRR Railroad Museum.

Left: National Route 66 Museum, Elk City, with one of Wanda Queenan's giant Kachina dolls outside.

Below: Cattle and Oklahoma are virtually synonymous.

Texola was once a lively place, but the coming of the Interstate has turned it into a ghost town, and most of its businesses — like the Longhorn Trading Post, a restaurant opened in the 1930s — have been abandoned for years. One recent traveler provided this eloquent description of what he saw there: "There's not much but a couple houses and the requisite derelict steel bodies, some with seized-up motors, some drawn and quartered for parts long ago...The highway

cuts through town like an old, nicked blade. Four lanes, divided, but the grass grows green and thickening through the many cracks in the two inside lanes. Only the rolling wheels of a few dozen cars and pickups a day keep the outside lanes cropped close." Texola provides a haunting final glimpse of Route 66 in Oklahoma; a few miles beyond what was once the town center, we cross into the Lone Star State.

Right: The timeworn sign for the Longhorn Trading Post in Texola.

VOICE OF THE ROAD →

I am willin' and anxious an' ready any day

To work for a decent livin', an' pay my honest way;

For I can earn my victuals, an' more too,

I'll be bound,

If any body only is willin' to have me round.

(from Farm Ballads *by Will Carleton, 1845–1912)*

Above: A migrant family photographed by Dorothea Lange.

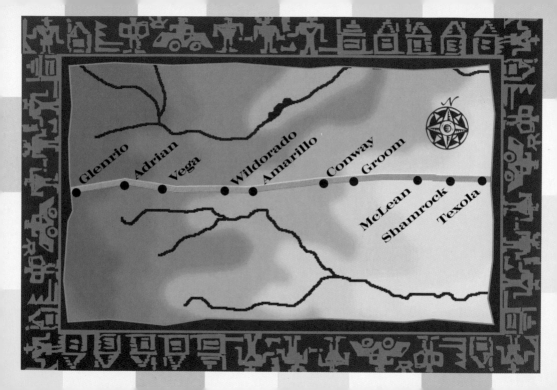

Texas

E arly travelers through Texas on Route 66 had considerable difficulties to face. In 1930, according to one witness (quoted in Susan Croce Kelly's *Route 66*), four wire gates blocked the road between Shamrock and Amarillo, and its surface was still ungraded and unpaved. It was not until 1938 that the state's entire 178-mile (286km) stretch of highway was concreted, saving drivers from hazards like the notorious Jericho Gap, near Groom, whose treacherous "gumbo soil" would turn the road into a mire in wet conditions. Beyond this former accident black spot (and a nearby stretch of road known as Death Alley) Route 66 continues via Amarillo to the now almost abandoned border town of Glenrio.

TEXAS

Landscape & Climate

The Texas Panhandle is a land of wide, unvarying plains stretching all the way to New Mexico. Temperatures reach 93°F (34°C) in summer, but the winter climate can be severe, as songwriter Bobby Troup recalls in Susan Croce Kelly's *Route 66*. "We ran into a snowstorm outside Amarillo: it was about eleven or twelve at night and absolutely blinding. I was really frightened." Another figure closely associated with the Old Road, Jack Rittenhouse (see page 258) describes hazards like the fierce winds that "bring sudden temperature drops and sometimes whip up clouds of sand," but also acknowledges the deep impression made on him by "the almost limitless emptiness of the countryside."

O highway I travel, do you say to me *Do not leave me?*

Do you say *Venture not — if you leave me you are lost?...*

O public road, I say back I am not afraid to leave you,

yet I love you,

You express me better than I can express myself,

You shall be more to me than my poem.

(from Song of the Open Road *by
Walt Whitman — 1819–1889)*

Only about 178 miles (286km) of Route 66 are in Texas. The road passes across a region known (due to its shape on the map) as the Panhandle, taking in the city of Amarillo as well as many smaller settlements bypassed by I-40 — which heads through the state in an almost straight, east-west line from Texola to Glenrio.

The first town encountered on the Old Road is Shamrock. Originally called Wheeler, it acquired its Irish name after an émigré sheep-farmer, George Nichols, christened his nearby homestead "Shamrock" to remind him of his roots in the Emerald Isle. The local railroad stop took up the name, and the town was officially incorporated as Shamrock in 1911. On St. Patrick's Day in 1938, when paving of 66 was completed in the area, Shamrock held a parade to celebrate, and this event has now become an annual tradition — during which all the local participants become temporarily "Irish!"

Left: The flag of Texas — a independent republic for nine years before joining the USA in 1845.

Over the years, Shamrock's Irishness
has grown steadily. The town's
Elmore Park boasts a piece of the
original Blarney Stone, brought from
Blarney Castle in Cork County, Eire, and
dedicated, during a ceremony in March
1959, to "The memory of good St.
Patrick, the spirit of good wholesome
fun, [...] the growth and prosperity of
Shamrock, Texas, and to the
wonderful people who dwell
within." There is also an Irish
Village, incorporating a gazebo and
murals, in the heart of the
downtown area.

Shamrock owed its "growth and prosperity" not only to St. Patrick, but also to its location at the intersection of two major highways: Route 66, running from east to west, and U.S. 83, stretching from Canada to Mexico. Travelers reaching the town often wanted food for themselves and gas for their vehicles, and on April 1, 1936, a striking new dual facility was opened to meet their needs: the Tower Station and U-Drop Inn.

Right: The Fina Tower gas station in Shamrock dates from 1936.

The U-Drop Inn, Shamrock

ROUTE 66

According to Shamrock's website, the U-Drop Inn's unique Art Deco design was conceived by its co-owner, John Nunn, who sketched its outline in the sand with a nail! The restaurant (run by Nunn and his wife) received a lot of praise after it opened in 1936: one local newspaper described it as "the swankiest of the swank eating places." Nunn's friend W.C. Tennison was the first owner/operator of the Fina service station attached to the U-Drop; both businesses continued to serve customers until the mid-1990s.

Leaving Shamrock, Route 66 passes through the small community of Lela, and then continues nine miles (14km) further west to McLean. In the 1940s, this once-bustling place had, according to the University of Texas Handbook of the state, "six churches, a newspaper, fifty-nine businesses, and a population of 1,521." The decline in the local oil industry, growth of other industrial centers, and decommissioning of Route 66 have all taken their toll on the

Left: McLean's Devil's Rope Museum.

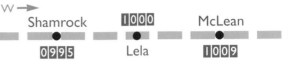

town, but it remains a worthwhile place to visit. Of especial interest is its Devil's Rope Museum, which examines the history of barbed wire — a seemingly mundane invention that transformed much of rural America. In the words of journalist Alistair Cooke, it "defined the prairie farmer's private property for the first time...and incidentally killed off the cowboy — or, rather, by denying him settled land as open range eventually turned him into a rancher, with his own domain fenced in."

Left: Another landmark in McLean — the town's Avalon movie theater.

During World War II, the Texas Panhandle played host to a group of temporary, involuntary settlers: German prisoners-of-war who were interned near McLean from 1943 to 1945. As Jessica L. Wooldridge explains in an article for *Route 66 Magazine*, the Panhandle, with its vast desert and sparse population, was felt to be an ideal location for captured enemy troops, and several other POW compounds were built elsewhere in the region. The McLean camp was designed to accommodate up to 3,000 prisoners; the first of them arrived in July 1943. They worked (for 80 cents a day) on local ranches, or cleaned up the streets of the town under armed guard, and caused few problems. During the two years the camp was in operation, there were only two (unsuccessful) escape attempts; and Wooldridge reports that for many years after the War "folks in McLean received letters from some of the prisoners…expressing their thanks for the kind treatment given them."

Left: Phillips gas station, McLean. The distinctive
"Phillips 66" logo incorporates the Route 66 shield.

1959 Cadillac Eldorado Seville 2-door hardtop

By 1959, Cadillacs were sporting the most sharply elevated tail fins in the company's history — a design soon to be immortalized at Texas' Cadillac Ranch! (see pages 218-219).

Below: Power steering and automatic transmission were standard.

The Eldorado Seville was an impressive, expensive ($7,400), and powerful car, with a 6.4 liter V8 engine and a top speed of 110mph (177kph). Its high performance was reflected in its heavy fuel consumption, which averaged as much as 14 miles to the gallon (20lit/100km).

W →

| 1009 | | Alanreed | | 1025 |
| McLean | | 1023 | | Jericho Gap |

Just down the road from McLean is Alanreed — once a larger town than its neighbor, but now with a population only in double figures. Its present layout dates from about 1900, and it is probably named after the partners in the contracting firm that built it, Alan and Reed.

In the past, the settlement had a slightly different location, about six miles (10km) from its current site, and a succession of other, more colorful names. These included Spring Tank, Prairie Dog Town, and, most famously, Gouge Eye — after a bar-room fight following which, according to Bob Moore and Patrick Grauwels in their *Illustrated Guidebook to the Mother Road,* two cowboys persuaded a passing traveler that fallen grapes from the buffet were eyes that had been gouged out during the melee.

Beyond Alanreed was the infamous, 18-mile (29km) Jericho Gap (see pages 184-185). The remains of Jericho itself can be reached via an exit off I-40.

Right: "66" Super Service Station,
Alanreed, built by Bradley Kiser in 1930.

W →

Jericho Gap   **1046**   Lark   **1058**   Amarillo
•   •   •   •   •
1025   Groom   **1050**   Conway   **1095**

I-40 continues towards Groom. At the turn-off that leads to the town
is the so-called "Leaning Tower of Texas" — a water tower
deliberately built at an angle to attract the attention of travelers!
Like many similar settlements, Groom was built around the
railroad tracks; it lies on the route of the famous Rock Island line,
and was formally incorporated in 1911. It grew throughout the
1920s and 1930s, thanks to an oil boom and the coming of Route
66, and was also a center for the storage and shipping of farm
produce — grain elevators can still be seen on the road leading
from Groom to Lark, about four miles (6.5km) further west. From
here, 66 completes the remaining 45-odd miles (72km) to Amarillo
via Conway. Palo Duro Canyon, shown in the photograph, lies a
little to the south of I-40 in this area, and is well worth making a
detour to visit.

Left: Palo Duro Canyon, south of Amarillo. Its walls tower
1,200 feet (366m) above the surrounding landscape.

Oh, Amarillo, what'd you want my baby for?

Oh, Amarillo, now he won't come home no more.

You done played a trick on me,

hooked him in the first degree,

Put in another quarter, push Dolly and then Porter,

While he racks up fifty thousand on the pinball machine.

(from Amarillo by Emmylou Harris and Rodney Crowell, 1975)

Left: Harley-Davidson jukebox
by Rock-Ola, 1994.

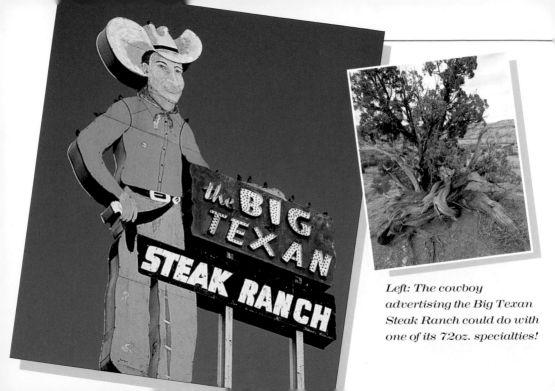

Left: The cowboy advertising the Big Texan Steak Ranch could do with one of its 72oz. specialties!

1095

Amarillo means "yellow" in Spanish; the town was originally called Oneida, but took its new name from a nearby lake and creek. By the late 1880s, it had a post office and a railroad freight service (the workers who laid the tracks for the Fort Worth and Denver City Railway were blamed for changing the Spanish pronunciation of "Amarillo" to its current "Americanized" version), and it quickly grew into one of the nation's busiest cattle-shipping points.

Amarillo was already an important railroad town (served by four separate companies) before the arrival of the highway. Although there were paved roads in some of its surrounding areas as early as 1922, concreting was not completed on the stretch of 66 east of the city (including the Jericho Gap) until the late 1930s. By then, Amarillo had become what its original developers had always intended it to be: the main center of trade and commerce for the entire Panhandle region.

Amarillo offers its visitors — especially those with hearty appetites — a truly Texan welcome. Diners can get a free 72oz. steak at The Big Texan Steak Ranch & Opry on I-40...as long as they can eat their meal (including shrimp cocktail, salad, bread, and baked potato) within an hour. 35,000 people have tried this since the restaurant opened in the 1950s; only 5,500 have succeeded. The Steak Ranch incorporates a motel for those who may need to rest after making the attempt!

There are many other interesting things to see in town, including the Amarillo Livestock Auction, which takes place every

Above: While not on 66, this display at Texas' Kilgore Oil Museum shows how rough the going was in the "old days."

Tuesday morning and attracts ranchers from all over the Panhandle; and the recently restored area around Sixth Avenue (between Georgia and Western Streets), with its antique shops, restaurants, and cafés. Outside the city are natural attractions such as the Lake Meredith National Recreation Area and the Palo Duro Canyon.

Left: Amarillo plays host to an important livestock auction.

They let me out on the streets of Amarillo, sixty miles from Pampa. I walked through town, and it got colder. Tumbleweeds, loose gravel, and dirt and beaten snow crawled along the streets and vacant lots, and the dust rolled in on a high wind, and fell on down across the upper plains. [...] A sign on a board said, Population, 50,000, Welcome.

(from Bound For Glory by Woody Guthrie, 1943)

Amarillo

1095

Undoubtedly the most striking sight on the road outside Amarillo is the Cadillac Ranch, established by Stanley Marsh 3, and featured on pages 218-219. Beyond it, the highway continues across the vast plains that stretch from here to New Mexico — the Spanish term for them is "llano estacado" ("staked plains": the name probably derives from early travelers' use of wooden stakes to mark out their path).

The railroads made inroads into this territory several decades before Route 66. In the early 1900s, the Chicago, Rock Island and Gulf company was planning a new line from Amarillo, and was granted a right-of-way through land owned by William Henry Bush about 14 miles (22.5km) west of the city. The town of Bushland grew up around the tracks, as did the next settlement on the road, Wildorado, which the Rock Island chose as a shipping point for the new line. The road and the now disused railtracks travel on from Wildorado to Vega, about 15 miles (24km) further west.

Right: Texas cowboys corral prime Texas cattle near Amarillo — a scene that has changed little over the years.

Vega — the name is Spanish for "plain" or "meadow" — has been settled for over a century. By the 1910s it was a flourishing railroad town, and in 1915 it became the county seat for Oldham County (which takes in nearly all the Western section of Route 66 in Texas from Wildorado to beyond Adrian). Despite a serious fire in 1931, Vega's economy continued to grow, and the paving of the highway through the town center (soon followed by the construction of tourist courts and other amenities)

Right: The blue bonnet, Texas' state flower, growing near Vega.

Below: One of the many cactuses that flourish in the Texan sun.

gave a further boost to its prosperity.

Vega and the neighboring town of Adrian owe a lot to the Mother Road; and in 1996 the communities expressed their gratitude with a major celebration of Route 66's 70th anniversary. This event, held halfway between the two settlements and attended by visitors from all over the USA, featured a calf-roping exhibition, automobile shows — and a Texas-sized barbecue!

Cadillac Ranch, Amarillo

ROUTE 66

The Cadillac Ranch, a group of ten Cadillacs buried, with their tailfins sticking up, on land outside Amarillo belonging to local helium tycoon Stanley Marsh 3, was created in 1974 by the Ant Farm – a trio of experimental artists comprising Chip Lord, Hudson B. Marquez, and Doug Michels. Their "site specific artwork" was conceived as a tribute to the Cadillac's classic design, and the featured cars range from a 1949 Club Coupé to a 1963 sedan.

As several seasoned Route 66 travelers have observed, simply tracking the path of the westerly section of the old road in Texas — let alone driving it — can sometimes be fraught with difficulties. Michael Wallis, in his *Route 66 — The Mother Road*, comments that "At many points...what was once Route 66 simply disappears and can't be found." Entire settlements have vanished too: once, there was a place called Ontario near Vega, but there is no trace of it now

Right: A rest-stop for a heavily-laden truck in Landergin.

W ➡

Vega
•

1139
•
Adrian

1124

— while a café
and filling station
are all that
remain of
Landergin, a once
busy work camp a
few miles farther
on. However, there
can be no
mistaking the city
limits of Adrian,

ILLINOIS • MISSOURI • KANSAS • OKLAHOMA
TEXAS • NEW MEXICO • ARIZONA • CALIFORNIA

ROUTE 66

THE MOTHER ROAD

about 15 miles (24km) west of Vega, where a large marker
proclaims the town as the mid-point of 66, and a smaller sign
carries a more cryptic message in multi-colored lettering:
"Adrian — you will never be the same."

According to the sign on the window of Adrian's appropriately named Midpoint Café, the town is 1,139 miles (1,833km) from both Chicago and Santa Monica. The Midpoint has been a landmark in Adrian — under various names — since the 1920s. Originally called Zella's, and occupying just one room with a dirt floor, it was expanded and redeveloped in the 1950s; photographs showing how it looked in earlier days can be seen on its walls.

Another famous place to eat in Adrian, the Bent Door Café, is currently closed; its former proprietors, Bob and Clara Gruhlkey, were inducted into the Texas Route 66 Hall of Fame in 1996. An article in the *Amarillo Globe-News* revealed that one of the couple's most memorable experiences during their years behind the counter was playing host to 28 boy scouts whose bus had broken down nearby: they gave the children a tour of Adrian, and laid on a barbecue for them in a local park.

Left inset: The Bent Door Café in Adrian, situated (as its window display proclaims) at the midway point of Route 66.

Chicken-Fried Steak with Texas Sauce

MAKES 4 SERVINGS

Chicken-fried steak is a staple throughout the Lone Star State, together with its traditional accompaniment, "Texas sauce:" the gravy made with fat in a skillet after a steak was fried. Like so many other specialties of this region, it was designed to satisfy the hearty appetites of ranchers and cattlemen. Ramon F. Adams recalls in *Come an' Get it, The Story of the Old Cowboy Cook*, that " No cowboy worthy of the calling wanted his steaks any way but fried."

1/4 cup all-purpose flour
1/2 teaspoon garlic salt
Pinch of cayenne pepper, or to taste

Freshly ground black pepper, to taste
4 steaks, such as sirloin, 6–8 ounces each and 1/2-inch thick

About 2 tablespoons vegetable oil or beef drippings
1 cup milk

Route Food

1. Combine the flour, garlic salt, cayenne pepper, and black pepper in a plastic bag and shake. Add the steaks, one at a time, shaking until lightly coated. Remove the steak from the bag and shake any excess flour back into the bag.

2. Heat the oil or melt the drippings in a large skillet over medium-high heat. Add the steaks to the pan and fry for 3 minutes on each side for rare, or 5 minutes on each side for well-done. Fry the steaks in batches if there is not enough room in the pan, keeping each fried steak warm in a low oven until they are all fried. Add extra oil or drippings to the pan as necessary.

Right: You expect a square meal in Texas, and usually you get it.

3. Meanwhile, to make the Texas sauce, empty the flour mixture remaining in the bag into a small bowl, and stir in 2 tablespoons of the milk to make a smooth paste.

4. When all the steaks have been fried, pour the milk paste into the pan, stirring to scrape up any crisp bits on the bottom. Lower the heat to medium and add the remaining milk, stirring continuously until the gravy thickens and bubbles.

5. Adjust the seasoning, if necessary. Serve the steaks with the Texas sauce, and pan-fried potatoes.

Adrian

1 1 3 9

Route 66 made travel easier for car owners and truckers — but people with no vehicles of their own also benefited from it, thanks to the growing number of long-distance buses serving the highway. By the 1950s, the Greyhound company's distinctive silver cruisers were a familiar sight on this stretch of 66; and Howard Suttle, a West Texas native who spent 28 years as a Greyhound driver in Texas, New Mexico, and Oklahoma, has recently written a book about his experiences. Appropriately titled *Behind the Wheel...On Route 66,* it describes some of the difficulties and dangers faced by himself and his colleagues, from bridge washouts and blizzards to lost or troublesome passengers. There are also more humorous anecdotes — like the story of what happened to the Greyhound that drove off on its own one day in Santa Rosa! Howard's stories bring to life an important and sometimes-overlooked aspect of highway history; more details about it are on pages 390-393.

*Right: Greyhound and other bus services
meant that everyone could enjoy Route 66.*

W →

1139
● Adrian

Glenrio
● **1159**

NEW MEXICO

The final 20-mile (32km) stretch of Route 66 in Texas runs from Adrian to the border settlement of Glenrio — never a large place, but a busy one until the decommissioning of the old road turned it into a virtual ghost town. Today, drivers could be forgiven for feeling some unease as they approach it: the Glenrio exit on I-40 is numbered 0; the Texas portion of the town (which straddles the state line) is in the strangely-named Deaf Smith County; and the entire area has an eerie, forgotten feel.

In the old days, Glenrio's divided status was potentially confusing for the traveler. Deaf Smith County was "dry", so the town's bars were on its New Mexico side — while the service stations were concentrated in Texas, where duty on gas was lower. But after the coming of I-40, there was little reason to stop there at all; although the deserted shops and motels are a reminder of how different things once were.

Left: At the border...the now bypassed town of Glenrio on the Texas/New Mexico stateline .

The V-twin was Crocker's last major motorcycle design. His hand-built machines were unable to compete in price against larger manufacturers.

1938 Crocker

Motorcycle designer Al Crocker, a former staffer at Indian, began to build bikes under his own name in the 1930s. At first, he concentrated on speedway racing, but by 1936 — encouraged by the growing viability of long-distance travel on Route 66 and other paved highways — he was turning his attention to creating a machine for the road. The result was the model shown here, which sported a lightweight body and a powerful 50 horsepower engine.

Left: This model sold for $550; fewer than 100 were made.

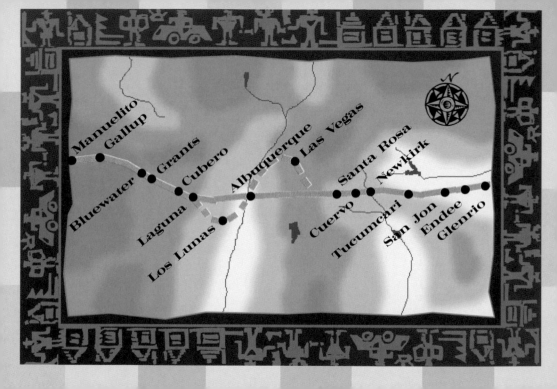

New Mexico

New Mexico, which occupies an area of 121,590 square miles (314,894km²), has been a part of the USA since only 1848, and a state since 1912. Hispanic explorers first laid claim to the territory in the sixteenth century; prior to their arrival, it had been inhabited and cultivated by Native Americans for some 10,000 years. From the border town of Glenrio, Texas, Route 66 stretches 375 miles (603km) west across New Mexico to Manuelito, then continues over the Arizona State line. Before 1937, it also took in the historic state capital, Santa Fe, but this northerly detour was subsequently abandoned in favor of a more direct path to Albuquerque and beyond, similar to that now followed by I-40.

Landscape & Climate

The plains landscape on the eastern stretch of Route 66 in New Mexico is almost identical to the Panhandle terrain in the neighboring state of Texas. Albuquerque, just over 200 miles (322km) from the border, is the largest city in the state. It has a mild climate, with temperatures rarely exceeding 93°F (34°C), and falling to a winter minimum of 22°F (-6°C). Further west, the scenery becomes more dramatic; the Acoma Pueblo ("Sky City") lies south of the highway near McCartys (about 60 miles [97km] beyond Albuquerque), while the San Mateo mountains are visible to the north. Near Thoreau, the road reaches its zenith, climbing to 7,275 feet (2,217m) at the point where it crosses the Continental Divide.

That's the end of Texas. New Mexico and the mountains. In the far distance, waved up against the sky, the mountains stood. And the wheels of the cars creaked around, and the engines were hot, and the steam spurted around the radiator caps.

(from The Grapes of Wrath *by John Steinbeck, 1939)*

Right: Going west — a family hitching a lift on Route 66 in the 1930s.

Below: The Café Diner, on the once busy highway through Glenrio.

SW → TEXAS
1159
● Glenrio
Endee
● **1164**
1170
● Bard

As we have seen, comparatively little of Route 66 was newly constructed or paved in its early days. In fact, large sections, especially in Western states like New Mexico, were simply "[existing] local roads...spliced together to create a makeshift highway," in the words of historian David Kammer. Modern travelers can get a taste of these old, rougher roads as soon as they enter the state; an unpaved portion of 66 still runs from Glenrio through Endee (five miles [8km] further west) to the remains of another, almost vanished settlement, Bard. This area was cowboy country, where heavy drinking and shootouts were so commonplace that the authorities in Endee would have a trench dug on Saturdays, ready to receive the bodies of unlucky gunslingers the following morning. Things are quieter now — but drivers preferring to bypass Endee and the dirt road surface of Old 66 can opt for the interstate, which leads more directly westward.

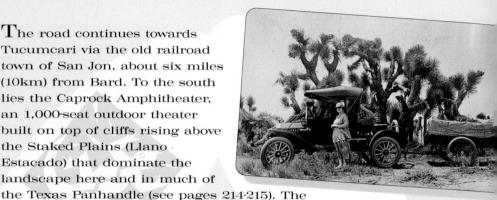

The road continues towards Tucumcari via the old railroad town of San Jon, about six miles (10km) from Bard. To the south lies the Caprock Amphitheater, an 1,000-seat outdoor theater built on top of cliffs rising above the Staked Plains (Llano Estacado) that dominate the landscape here and in much of the Texas Panhandle (see pages 214-215). The Amphitheater is used for a variety of plays and pageants; one recent show mounted there was based on the life of outlaw gunman Billy the Kid (William H. Bonney, 1859—81), who is buried near Fort Sumner, about 50 miles (80km) south of Tucumcari.

Above: An early traveler takes a break from the rigors of the road, c. 1920.

W →

Bard

1170

1176

San Jon

Tucumcari

1199

Tucumcari itself was once an important stopover on Route 66 in New Mexico. Huge signs encouraged weary travelers to make their temporary destination "Tucumcari tonite," but today, only a fraction of the "2,000 rooms" advertised on the old billboards still exist. However, one famous motel remains in business there: the Blue Swallow, featured on the next two pages.

Above: One of the many roadside motel signs on the way to Tucumcari.

BLUE SWALLOW MOTEL

The Blue Swallow opened in 1942, and was acquired 16 years later by a local trailer park owner, Floyd Redman, who gave it to his fiancée, Lillian, as a wedding present. Over the next four decades, Mrs. Redman made the hotel an oasis of homespun hospitality, endearing it – and herself – to generations of guests. Although Lillian is now deceased, the Blue Swallow's new owners, Dale and Hilda Bakke, have pledged to preserve its unique atmosphere and classic décor.

Tucumcari

1199

Tucumcari today is a very different place from the wild early 20th century "tent city" that provided workers building the Chicago, Rock Island and Pacific Railroad (and numerous hangers-on) with rough accommodation and rowdy drinking-

places. Several accounts of the town's history mention its ominous nickname during this period: "Six-Shooter Siding." Before the arrival of the railroad it was known as Douglas, and was a smaller settlement, attracting local ranchers and farmers who came to buy provisions. But its

Above: This sculpture, with its huge numerals standing out against the sky, is in Tucumcari.

position at the "gateway to New Mexico" brought growing numbers of travelers — first by rail, later by road — and by 1946, Jack Rittenhouse (see pages 258-259) author of the first-ever guide book to Route 66, was able to remark that "Tucumcari is quite a tourist center."

It remains an interesting place to stay, eat, and shop — with stores such as Tepee Curios (selling jewelry and gifts made by Native Americans) and a wide range of diners, cafés, and bars.

SW →

| Tucumcari | 1220 | Newkirk | 1241 | Santa Rosa |

1199 · Montoya · 1232 · Cuervo · 1258

A few miles outside Tucumcari lies another stretch of Old 66 — a scenic route passing through Montoya (site of Richardson's store and gas station, which has been serving travelers since 1942), and westward via Newkirk and Cuervo to Santa Rosa. For many years, roads around this town were graced by a distinctive billboard image: the Fat Man, whose smiling face attracted thousands of hungry motorists to the Club Café, home of the best biscuits and gravy in the southwest. Sadly, the café was forced to close in the early 1990s. However, the rights to the Fat Man logo were subsequently acquired by Joseph Campos and his wife Christina, owners of Joseph's Cantina on Santa Rosa's Will Rogers Drive, close to the site of the old Club Café. The frontage at Joseph's now displays the famous sign, and the Fat Man is now directing a new generation of Route 66 customers to the restaurant.

The original Club Café in Santa Rosa, which opened in 1935, and was famous for its "Fat Man" adverts.

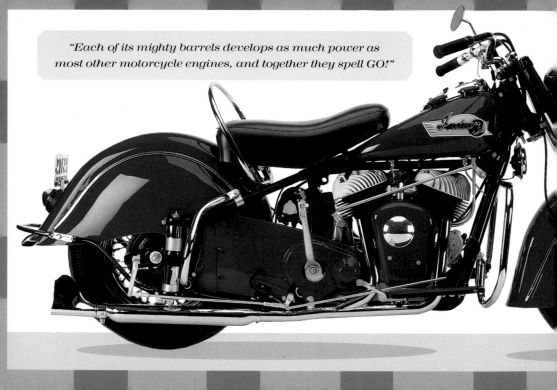

"Each of its mighty barrels develops as much power as most other motorcycle engines, and together they spell GO!"

1953 Indian Chief

The Indian Chief, introduced in 1946, was a new bike for a new era. Ex-servicemen — many of whom had previously traveled Route 66 in military convoys during World War II — could now explore the highway for themselves. The Chief, with its elegant outline, swooping fenders, low fuel consumption, and competitive price tag, offered them a stylish and economical ride.

Above: The "Eighty" stands for 80 cubic inches — 1310cc.

LA BAJADA HILL, BETWEEN SANTA FE AND ALBUQUERQUE, NEW MEXICO

Originally, the road beyond Santa Rosa, instead of continuing in an east-west line, made a north-westerly detour to Las Vegas, then headed for Santa Fe, descended La Bajada Hill (see photograph) and went south through Albuquerque to Los Lunas before finally turning west again. As Sue Bohannon Mann reports in an article for *Route 66 Magazine*, early moves to bypass this indirect route were made by New Mexico State governor, A.T. Hannett. In 1926, he gave orders for a "new cutoff [that] would connect the road seven miles west of Santa Rosa to an existing highway from Moriarty on into

Above: Old postcard view of La Bajada Hill, on Route 66's Santa Fe loop.

[Albuquerque]." Hannett's 69-mile (111km) dirt road reduced the mileage between Santa Rosa and Albuquerque from 195 miles (314km) to 114 (183km), taking a similar direction to the later, paved highway that officially replaced Route 66's "Santa Fe loop" in 1937. Beyond Moriarty, 66 climbs from Barton to the 7,000ft (2,134m) summit of Sedillo Hill, and down through the spectacular Tijeras Canyon towards Albuquerque.

This photograph, dating from the 1920s, shows the early winding road from La Bajada down to Albuquerque.

LOS ANGEL
790 MILES

CHICAGO
1,345 MILES

Route 66 runs through Albuquerque as the city's Central Avenue — a long street lined with motels, restaurants, and other businesses, some of them dating back to the road's early days. However, one major attraction on Central, the 66 Diner, is not quite what it may seem. Although housed in a genuine 1940s Phillips gas station, the diner itself is a modern, highly effective replica of an old-style eaterie, offering a combination of tradition — old photos on the walls, old tunes on the jukebox, classic dishes on the menu — and some zany contemporary touches. Two recent visitors, Roger and Jane Holm, reported that "all of the servers [there had] taken on the personae of cartoon characters — from their nicknames to their haircuts." The overall impression, though, remains solidly nostalgic ("lots of neon and 50s music") and the restaurant is a huge success not only with travelers but also with Albuquerque's own residents.

Left: One of the most popular eating places in Albuquerque, the 66 Diner.

Travelin' down this lonesome road,

My old guitar is my load.

I am a thousand miles from home,

I'm out in the western states alone.

I got them old Hitch Hike Blues,

I done wore out my shoes.

(from Hitch Hike Blues, *an old American folk song)*

Right: Headstock of a Stromberg Master 400 guitar, 1948.

Albuquerque

1372

Albuquerque is often known as Duke City, after the Spanish Viceroy Francisco Fernandez de la Cueva, Duke of Alburquerque (sic), for whom the original settlement was named in the early 18th century. The first "r" in Alburquerque was dropped in the years after America took over the region in 1846; one popular myth suggests that the old name was too long to fit on signs for the railroads, which arrived there in 1880.

Half a century later, the city's economy received a further boost from the advent of the new highway — and in the light of this, it seems fitting that Albuquerque should eventually have become the home of Jack Rittenhouse, 66's first systematic chronicler. His 1946 *Guidebook to Route 66*, compiled after countless journeys up and down the road in a 1939 American Bantam coupé (at an average speed of 35mph/56kph!), remains fascinating reading. Rittenhouse died in 1991, two years after his guide was republished in its original format.

Right: Albuquerque by night; and (insets) a sculpture from the Indian Cultural Center, and the El Vado Motel sign.

W →

Albuquerque

1372

1381

Nine Mile Hill

Route 66 crosses the Rio Grande on Albuquerque's Old Town Bridge, and leaves the city behind as it ascends Nine Mile Hill, whose summit is precisely nine miles (14km) from the center of town. However, travelers wanting to take a closer look at the nearby landscape should leave I-40 at Exit 254 (Unser Boulevard) and head

for the Petroglyph National Monument. This area, which includes Boca Negra Canyon, is part of the West Mesa escarpment, described by James Sentell in *Route 66 Magazine* as "a seventeen-mile long lava-carved prominence containing more than fifteen-thousand rock engravings (given the technical term petroglyphs) and scores of archaeological sites." Some of the engravings,

Above: Heavy traffic on Nine Mile Hill, west of Albuquerque.

Below: A nearby mural shows the highway stretching across the desert.

showing animals, humans, and symbols, are over 3,000 years old; they and their surrounding terrain can be explored on walking trails (of varying lengths and levels of strenuousness) organized by the National Park Service.

KiMo Theater, Albuquerque

The KiMo Theater, whose Pueblo Deco design combines Native American and Art Deco influences, dates from 1927. It was commissioned by a local Italian-American businessman, Oreste Bachechi, and built by the Boller Brothers of Kansas City, who were responsible for many other fine theaters throuhgout the Southwest. Its interior, decorated with Navajo-style carvings, also features seven panoramic murals. The KiMo is undergoing restoration, but will reopen in 2000.

W →

1381
●
Nine Mile Hill

Rio Puerco
■
●
1391

A short distance beyond the top of Nine Mile Hill is the Rio Puerco, a tributary of the Rio Grande, and the site of an historic road bridge over Route 66. The structure (no longer open to traffic) is a "Parker truss" design; bridges of this type were built by a number of contractors from the late 19th century onwards, and were sometimes (although not in this case) supplied from a catalog as a prefabricated kit. Other Parker trusses can be seen as far afield as Wisconsin and Mississippi, but this one, built in 1933 and remodeled in 1957, is the longest single span example in New Mexico, measuring 250 feet (76m), and constructed from ten 25-foot (7.6) panels. According to the state's Route 66 Association, it has recently been nominated for inclusion on the National Register of Historic Places, which should result in its permanent preservation. In the foreground of the picture is a recently constructed roadside coffee shop.

Right: At the Rio Puerco. The historic Parker truss bridge can be seen beyond the coffee shop.

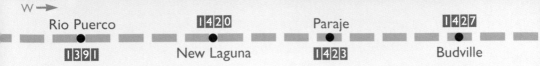

W →

Rio Puerco
1391
1420
New Laguna
Paraje
1423
1427
Budville

For the next 50-odd miles (80km), the road is surrounded by the Laguna and Acoma Native American Reservations. About 25 miles (40km) beyond the Rio Puerco is Correo, once the collection and delivery point for postal services in the surrounding area — its name is Spanish for "mail." The next towns on this stretch of 66 are Mesita and, a little further west, Old Laguna — site of the famous church of St. Joseph, built by Franciscan friars from stone and adobe in 1705, and still in regular use today. New Laguna lies nearby, and the highway then continues past Paraje to Budville. This small settlement was named for Bud Rice, whose father founded a highly successful service station and towing company there in 1928. In 1967, according to Bob Moore and Patrick Grauwels in their *Illustrated Guidebook to the Mother Road*, Bud was murdered during a hold-up; his widow Flossie continued to run the business until 1979, when it finally closed.

Left: The Budville Trading Company, with a vintage gas pump on its forecourt, and vacant signboard.

I'm goin' down this road feelin' bad,
Lord, I'm goin' down this road feelin' bad,
Well, I'm goin' down this road feeelin' bad, Lord, Lord,
An' I ain't gonna be treated thisaway.

I ain't got but one old lousy dime,
Lord, I ain't got but one old lousy dime,
Well, I ain't got but one old lousy dime, Lord, Lord,
But I'll find me a new dollar some old day.

(American folk song)

Above: A family on the road during the Great Depression.

Righ: Santa María de Acoma, McCartys.

Two miles (3.2km) from Budville is Vila de Cubero: Nobel prizewinning novelist Ernest Hemingway (1899—1961) stayed at a roadside inn here while he was writing *The Old Man and the Sea*. The 11,300ft (3,444m) peak of Mount Taylor is visible from the highway, which passes through San Fidel before reaching McCartys. For many years, a Whiting Bros. gas station, motel, and restaurant stood here; at one time, the company, run by four brothers from Arizona, had no fewer than 44 franchises between Shamrock, Texas and Barstow, California. Recently, the McCartys premises were damaged by fire, revealing part of the Chief's Rancho Café, mentioned by Jack Rittenhouse in his 1946 Route 66 guide, and later hidden by the Whiting development. McCartys also features a fine Spanish Colonial-style church, dating from 1933. From here, it is only a few miles to Grants, a significant center for travelers since its foundation, as a railroad town, in 1881.

Left: This ATSF caboose, photographed at Grants, is a reminder of the town's close links with the railroad.

NW →

| 1446 | Milan | 1459 |
| Grants | 1452 | Bluewater |

The section of Route 66 around Grants runs through the black beds of lava known as the Malpais (Spanish for "badlands"). About 25 miles (40km) southwest of the town, these form a series of "ice caves" whose interiors, insulated by the lava, remain perpetually below freezing point — even when outside temperatures climb to 100° Fahrenheit (38°C). The caves are well worth a visit, as is El Morro, the famous "Inscription Rock" located near the town. This sandstone cliff bears petroglyphs, messages and graffiti left by Native Americans and other settlers and visitors over many centuries. Further information about both the Ice Caves and El Morro can be found on pages 390-393.

Just outside Grants is a relatively recent settlement on the path of Route 66: Milan, which was founded in the 1950s. About seven miles (11km) beyond it lies Bluewater, site of the "Route 66 Swap Meet" owned and run by Thomas Lamance.

Right: El Morro (the Inscription Rock) and (inset) a roadside billboard advertising Indian craftware.

INDIAN
VILLAGE
6
MILES

INDIAN HANDMADE
JEWELRY
STERLING SILVER
TURQUIOSE

Designed by Pontiac's chief engineer, John DeLorean, the GTO Judge had a 400 cubic inch Ram-Air engine that pushed the car to 60mph (97kph) in six seconds.

1969 Pontiac GTO Judge

The GTO Judge was aimed at power-hungry young drivers — and by the late 1960s, there were thousands of miles of freeway on which it could be put through its paces with the gas pedal hard down.

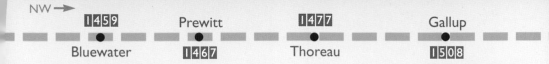

NW ➔

| 1459 | Prewitt | 1477 | Gallup |

Bluewater   1467   Thoreau   1508

After leaving Bluewater, 66 heads for Prewitt, a small settlement about eight miles (13km) to the west. Beyond it lies Thoreau — named for the writer Henry David Thoreau (1817–1862), although he had no direct connection with the town. The road now approaches North America's Continental Divide; at 7,275 feet (2,217m) above sea level, the highest elevation on the highway.

About 31 miles (50km) west along Route 66 is the city of Gallup, whose beautiful El Rancho Hotel has played host to many leading movie stars since it opened in 1937. Errol Flynn allegedly rode his horse into the bar while staying there; and signed photos of hundreds of other notable guests are on display inside the inn, which has recently been restored, and now provides motel accommodation in addition to its original, more spacious guest quarters. It continues to offer, in the words of its memorable slogan, "the charm of yesterday, and convenience of tomorrow."

Left: The southwestern section of the illustrated plan of Route 66 shown on pages 60-61.

Gallup offers a wide range of attractions to its visitors. The city has often described itself as "the Indian Capital of the United States," and is a major center for Native American art and jewelry, which can be bought at trading posts all over town. Other styles of art and architecture — from the 1928 El Morro Theater on Coal Avenue to "Paso po aqui," the giant construction of rock, glass, and steel created by Charles Mallery and Robert Hymer that

Right: Free-form jazz? Gallup's extraordinary "Bebop Sculpture."

SW →

Gallup

1512

Mentmore

1524

ARIZONA

1508

Allison

1516

Manuelito

overlooks downtown
Gallup — provide
something for all tastes;
and among the area's
many other attractions is
the annual hot air balloon
rally held in Red Rock
State Park, east of the
town, which attracts
hundreds of visitors.

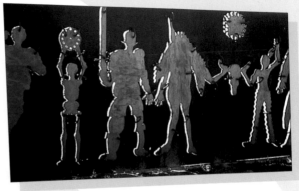

Gallup is also, of course,
the last major urban center
on Route 66 in New Mexico. The remaining 25-odd (40km) miles
of road in the state lead west through Allison, Mentmore, and
Manuelito, before finally crossing into Arizona.

*Above: Part of the "People's Sculpture,"
also on display in Gallup.*

Easy Pork Burritos

MAKES 4-6 SERVINGS

Burritos, like many other staples of Mexican cookery, spread quickly throughout the Southwest and eventually across the entire USA. Tasty, meaty finger-food, they are ideal for eating on the move. This recipe is quick, easy, and delicious — a traveler's delight.

4—6 large flour tortillas

2—3 tablespoons vegetable oil

1 onion, coarsely chopped

1 red or green bell pepper, chopped

1 garlic clove, minced

1 1/2 pounds boneless pork loin, cut into thin strips

Salt and cayenne pepper, to taste

1/2 teaspoon ground cumin

1 (11-ounce) can sweetcorn kernels, drained

1 (14-ounce) can red kidney beans, drained (optional)

2 ripe tomatoes, chopped

Route Food

TO SERVE

A choice of accompaniments such as bottled taco sauce,
sliced avocado, sliced red onion, shredded lettuce, grated
Monterey Jack cheese, and sour cream

1. Preheat the oven to 350°F. Stack the flour tortillas on a large
sheet of foil and wrap tightly. Put on a baking sheet and heat in the
oven for about 15 minutes.

2. Meanwhile, in a large, heavy-bottomed skillet or wok over
medium-high heat, heat 2 tablespoons of the oil. Add the onion, bell
pepper, and garlic and stir-fry for 2—3 minutes, until the vegetables
just begin to soften. Spoon onto a plate and set aside. Add the pork
to the pan and stir-fry for about 3 minutes, until golden and just
cooked, Season with the salt, cayenne, and ground cumin. Return
the cooked vegetables to the pan and add the corn kernels, beans, if

Right: Washing up after a meal remains a chore
even when it's finger food like easy pork burritos!

using, and tomatoes. Stir fry for another 2–3 minutes, until the pork is cooked through and the flavors are blended.

3. Lay the warmed tortillas on a work surface and divide the mixture evenly among the tortillas near one edge. Top each with a selection of the accompaniments. Fold the edge nearest the filling up and over the filling, just to cover the filling. Fold the two sides over to form an open envelope shape. Serve with extra taco sauce, if you like.

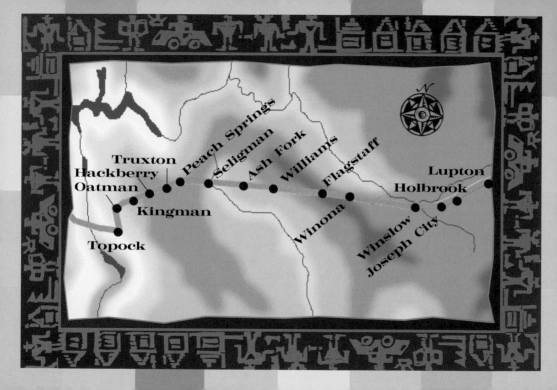

Arizona

Like New Mexico, Arizona was a former Mexican territory (its name comes from the Spanish for "dry zone" — *arrida-zona*); it became a state in 1912. Before the advent of Route 66, the Santa Fe railroad had been Arizona's main transporter of freight and passengers, and the highway leading west from Holbrook is dotted with settlements that originally grew up around its tracks. The 400-odd miles (644km) of Route 66 in Arizona were not fully paved until the mid-1930s, but the road quickly brought an influx of new travelers — some of them vacationers visiting attractions such as the Petrified Forest, others workers or migrants seeking a new life beyond the California border.

ARIZONA

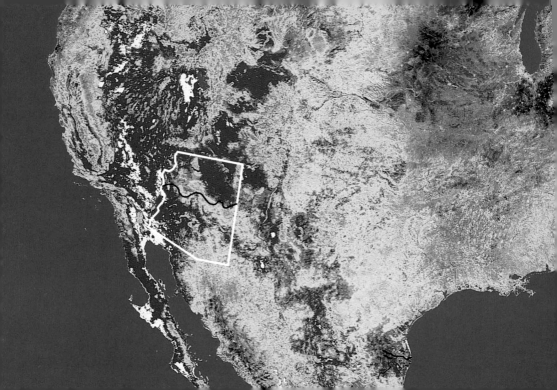

Landscape & Climate

Route 66's journey through Arizona gives travelers a taste of almost everything the region has to offer — except for the extremes of climate encountered in areas like the state capital, Phoenix, where daytime temperatures of up to 122°F (50°C) are not unknown. The road takes in Native American lands, geological phenomena like the Painted Desert and Petrified Forest described on pages 292-293, and the pines and mountain peaks around the city of Flagstaff — only 30 miles (48km) away from Williams, gateway to the Grand Canyon. Another site worth making a detour to see is Old London Bridge, installed at Lake Havasu City, about 20 miles (32km) south of where 66 crosses into California.

VOICE OF THE ROAD ➡

Well I'm standin' on a corner

In Winslow, Arizona

With such a fine sight to see

It's a girl, my Lord,

In a flat-bed Ford

Slowin' down to take a look at me.

(from Take It Easy *by Jackson Browne and Glenn Frey, 1972)*

Right: A corner in Winslow , Arizona, 1950s vintage.

The first section of Route 66 in Arizona passes across the southeast edge of the Navajo Indian Reservation — or the Navajo Nation, as most of its Native American residents prefer to call it. This vast area (it is larger than West Virginia) is home to 260,000 people, and its most famous landmark, Window Rock, is about 20 miles (32km) north of where the highway crosses the state line near Lupton. Lupton itself, originally a railroad and cattle town, now makes most of its money selling Navajo-made goods and souvenirs to visitors, via outlets like the Chief Yellowhorse Trading Post — positioned on Grants Road, within easy reach of I-40. The Old Road continues via Sanders and Chambers towards the city of Navajo, about 30

Right: A 1930 AAA Route 66 map and (far right) an abandoned stretch of 66 in Arizona.

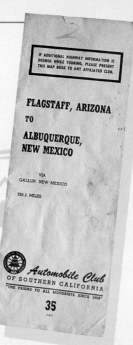

IF ADDITIONAL HIGHWAY INFORMATION IS DESIRED WHILE TOURING, PLEASE PRESENT THIS MAP BOOK TO ANY AFFILIATED CLUB.

FLAGSTAFF, ARIZONA
TO
ALBUQUERQUE, NEW MEXICO

VIA
GALLUP, NEW MEXICO

328.5 MILES

Automobile Club
OF SOUTHERN CALIFORNIA
"THE FRIEND TO ALL MOTORISTS SINCE 1900"

35

SW ➜

NEW MEXICO

1536
●
Lupton

Chambers
●
1559

1567
●
Navajo

miles (48km) southwest; nearby are Navajo Springs, where Arizona
was established as a Territory in 1863 — only 15 years after the US
had gained control of it as a result of the Mexican War.

SW →

Navajo

1609

1567

Holbrook

Approximately 15 miles (24km) west of Navajo is the entrance to the Petrified Forest National Park, set up to protect the amazing geological and archaeological features of this area. A 27-mile (43km) scenic drive through the park takes in areas where dead trees, washed into the lakes that once covered this region, became buried in layers of silt that prevented them from rotting. Over millions of years, they were transformed into crystallised quartz: a forest literally turned to stone. Toward the north of the park site, there are views into the nearby Painted Desert, with its richly colored earth and rocks created by the gradual erosion of ancient lake beds. The Park also features the excavated remains of a number of Native American sites, as well as the famous Newspaper Rock, which bears petroglyphs dating back thousands of years.

Further information about the Park and its Rainbow Forest Museum can be found on pages 390-393.

Right: Native American dwellings and fortifications carved out of an Arizona cliff face a few miles south of Route 66.

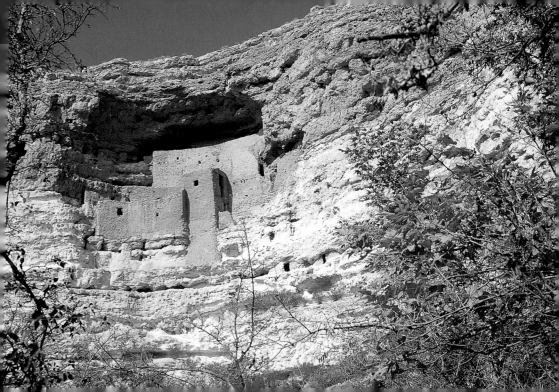

Wigwam Village, Holbrook

ROUTE 66

Motels offering accommodation in concrete teepees first appeared in the 1940s; and when Holbrook resident Chester E. Lewis saw one in Kentucky, he decided to build a similar establishment in his home town. After selecting a suitable site on West Hopi Drive, he acquired blueprints for the "tents," and undertook most of the construction work himself. Lewis's Wigwam Village opened in 1950; it is still run by his family, and has recently been refurbished.

Holbrook

1609

Like many similar settlements, Holbrook owed its early prosperity to cattle and railroads, but had to face the problems caused by a frequent influx of rowdy, hard-drinking laborers and cowmen. The city's often turbulent history is set out in its Museum, located in the old Navajo County Courthouse, built in 1898; the former County Jail, dating from the same period, is also open to visitors.

However, the railroads also brought respectable tourists, many of them en route to attractions like the Petrified Forest. New businesses quickly developed to serve them, including a restaurant housed in a string of

Left: Strawberry cactuses favor arid regions such as Arizona.

Left: An illuminated roadside café sign near Holbrook. The opening of Route 66 brought many visitors in its wake.

railroad boxcars, managed by an Englishman, Fred Harvey. Other "Harvey Houses" subsequently opened throughout the Southwest, becoming a byword for their quality and service (see pages 302-303); and with the arrival of the highways, the motel trade soon made an early appearance in Holbrook: one of the first-ever tourist camps is believed to have been opened here in the 1920s.

Just west of I-40 outside Holbrook is another of the city's attractions: the Hidden Cove Golf Course, described as "an oasis of green in the red rock terrain." Beyond it, the highway continues towards the little settlement of Joseph City, which was originally known as Allen's Camp, and dates back to 1876 — making it the longest-established community in Navajo County.

A few miles down the road, a pile of debris is all that remains of Ella's, a once flourishing retail business that used to sport signs proclaiming it "The First Trading Post on Route 66". The picture opposite shows how the abandoned store looked before its demolition. There is a sharp and poignant contrast between the ruins of Ella's and the remarkable success of another nearby trading post, the Jackrabbit: a Route 66 institution so famous that it can announce itself with just a symbol and a 3-word message: "Here It Is."

Left: Ella's Frontier Trading Post, Joseph City.
The building has now been completely demolished.

Jackrabbit Trading Post

The Jackrabbit was built in 1947 by two local entrepreneurs, Robbie Robinson and James Taylor – who were also responsible for creating the billboard campaign that has been so successful in spreading its fame among travelers. The trading post has changed hands a number of times, but retains a perennial appeal for tourists. Its present owners, Antonio and Cindy Jaquez, stock everything from soda, toys, and trinkets to yellow "Jackrabbit" underwear carrying its famous symbol!

Winslow, a few miles west of the
Jackrabbit Trading Post, began to
take its present form when the
railroad reached it in 1881. Edward
F. Winslow, for whom it was named,
was Vice-President of the Atlantic
and Pacific line — later acquired by
the Santa Fe, which proved to have
ambitious plans for the city.

Since 1908, the railroad had been
working in partnership with the
Fred Harvey Company (see pages
296-297) to build luxury hotels
adjacent to stations. In Winslow, the
Harvey/Santa Fe team surpassed

*Right: La Posada Hotel, opened in
1930, was designed by Mary Colter.*

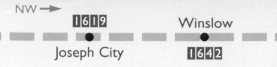

itself, creating a Spanish Colonial rancho-style station and hotel, La Posada, which opened in 1930. Staffed by the famous Harvey Girls (smart, impeccably trained catering staff largely recruited from the Eastern states) the inn was highly successful at first; but the post-war reduction in rail travel led to its eventual closure in 1957. However, unlike some other notable Harvey/Santa Fe hotels, La Posada has survived, and is now in business again under new management.

Right: Winslow's Tonto Drive-In movie theater and its snack bar.

On the western side of Winslow are the remains of the old Tonto drive-in movie theater; sadly, it seems that working examples of such facilities are now the exception rather than the rule.

In contrast, the next major landmark on the journey west is not a man-made ruin, but the result of a catastrophic natural event — the fall of a huge meteorite, which struck the ground some 10 miles (16km) from Meteor City about 50,000 years ago. The actual Meteor Crater site is off the highway; the crater itself, which is 550 feet (168m) deep, and 2.4 miles (3.9km) in circumference, can be viewed from a nearby Visitors'

Left: These huge wooden carvings are the main attraction in Twin Arrows,

NW →

Winslow   1654   Twin Arrows   1684

1642   Meteor City   1674   Winona

Center, which also organizes guided hikes around its rim. The Center's other attractions include a

Museum of Astrogeology and Astronaut Hall of Fame; more details about it are provided on pages 390-393.

Beyond Meteor Crater, the road heads on towards Winona, passing by the trading post at Twin Arrows before reaching the town.

Left: Meteor Crater is large enough to accommodate twenty football fields.

VOICE OF THE ROAD →

> **Flagstaff, Arizona,**
> **don't forget Winona...**
>
> *(from* Route 66 *by Bobby Troup, 1946)*

The late Bobby Troup urged us not to forget Winona in his classic song, *(Get Your Kicks On) Route 66,* but although it was once a fairly busy settlement, there is now little left to remember it by. The road rushes on past it towards Flagstaff, 16 miles (26km) to the west.

Before the arrival of highways or railroads, Flagstaff was already an important staging post for wagon trains en route to California. The city, which took its name from a tall, flag-decked pine tree often used as a position marker by early travelers, was formally established in 1876. Today, it is a prime location for business and

Above: The Museum Club — one of Flagstaff's most popular live music venues.

entertainment. Its top music venues include the Museum Club — a classic roadhouse that features its original owner's collection of stuffed animals mounted in tree branches above the dance floor! Voted "Readers' Favorite Dance Club" by *Country America* magazine, it is highly popular with a wide range of audiences and musicians.

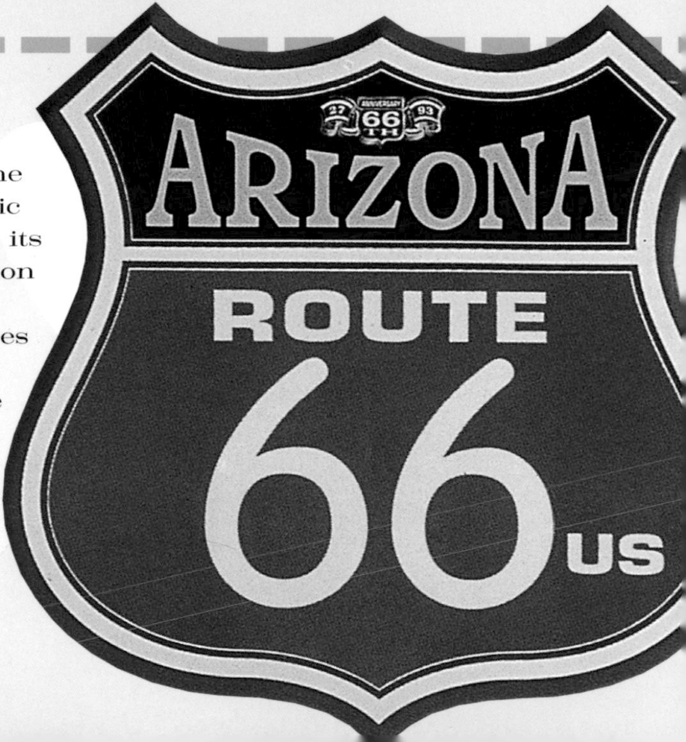

ARIZONA

27 66 93
ANNIVERSARY

ROUTE

66

US

From east of Winona to beyond Williams, the highway passes through more than 50 miles (80km) of forest. Williams itself, about 35 miles (56km) from Flagstaff, was, on October 13, 1984, the last place on the Old Road to be bypassed by the new Interstate. During the ceremony held to mark the occasion, which was attended by

Bobby Troup and other notables, one devotee (quoted in Michael Wallis' *Route 66 — The Mother Road*) was heard to remark that "The road is like Elvis Presley: it just won't die." The same is certainly true of Williams, whose flourishing downtown district is listed in the National Register for Historic Places,

Left: The Grand Canyon Hotel, Williams, in days of yore.

and includes elegant restaurants and stores, as well as a number of classic 1940s motels still boasting their original neon signs.

Williams is also the starting point for excursions to the surrounding Kaibab National Forest — and of course, the terminus for the Grand Canyon Railway, featured on pages 314-315.

Above: One of the many businesses in Williams selling Native American ware.

The Town & Country was powered by Chrysler's C-39 Spitfire 8-cylinder engine.

1948 Chrysler Town & Country

The post-war era saw a substantial increase in the number of private motorists using Route 66 and other major roads — and a new look to many of their vehicles. Among the most striking automobile designs of the period was Chrysler's Town and Country range, with their unique wood-bodied sides. Before World War II, wood had generally only been used on station wagons.

W →

Williams

1735

Grand Canyon

Ash Fork

1755

The Grand Canyon National Park lies about 65 miles (105km) north of Williams, and every year thousands of visitors travel there on the Grand Canyon Railway — which operates daily from its Williams Depot, built in 1908. Adjacent to it was the Fray Marcos Hotel, another collaboration between the Santa Fe Railroad and the Harvey Company (see pages 296-297 and 302-303). Its original dining room houses a Railroad Museum, displaying a range of historic artefacts and photos; while a new Fray Marcos Hotel offers modern accommodation combined with traditional Harvey style.

At the Grand Canyon end of the line, the train terminates at a log-built depot in the heart of the National Park's Historic District. This building, dating from 1909—10, is the only surviving structure of its kind still in use on an operational railroad. Coach tours from the depot provide visitors with an opportunity to explore the breathtaking surrounding area more fully.

Left: One of the most spectacular sights in the world, Grand Canyon National Park attracts more than 5,000,000 visitors every year.

Beyond Williams, the highway leads on to Ash Fork — first a stagecoach depot and later a stop on the Santa Fe. The town was once famous for its Harvey House

Hotel, the Escalante (opened in 1907, but now demolished); however, today it is best known as the "Flagstone Capital of the World," with six stoneyards shipping the locally mined slabs throughout the USA.

Seligman, 30 miles (48km) away, takes its name from Jesse Seligman, the banker who financed the construction of the Atlantic and Pacific Railway in the area. The town

Left: Seligman's Snow Cap drive-in restaurant is famous for its zany menu.

NW →
Williams
1735
1755
Ash Fork
Seligman
1785

developed beside it, and despite a chronic shortage of water (Paul Taylor, writing in *Route 66 Magazine*, describes how this was brought "in tank cars from Del Rio 'Puro' near Chino Valley...[and] delivered to homes at 50¢ a barrel"), it soon became an important center for livestock transportation and other business. Seligman, with its Historic Route 66 Visitor Center, is a worthwhile stopping point on the journey west.

Left: The Copper Cart Café in Seligman provides classic American food, as well as high-fiber, low-fat dishes.

Route Food

ROU

66

Ham Steaks with Red-Eye Gravy

MAKES 2 SERVINGS

One of the traditional southern truckstop recipes is a simply grilled or fried ham steak, served with a dark-tinged gravy (the color comes from the ham stock to which left-over black coffee is added).

2 fully-cooked ham
   steaks or slices
   cooked country ham,
   about 1/4-inch thick

1/2 cup black coffee

1 teaspoon brown
   sugar

*Right: Hotel Beale, a cool
   place in Kingman.*

Route Food

1. Using kitchen scissors or a sharp knife, cut off any rind from the ham and discard. Trim the excess fat, leaving a narrow margin. Reserve about 1 tablespoon of the clean white fat. Snip the edges of the steaks or slices.

2. Put the reserved fat in a heavy iron skillet and heat over medium heat until the fat melts and begins to splutter. Add the ham steaks or slices and cook for 2-3 minutes, until golden. Turn and cook the other side for about 2 minutes more, until brown. Remove to a plate and keep warm. Remove any solid pieces of fat.

3. Add the coffee and sugar to the pan and bring to a boil, stirring up any browned bits from the bottom. Simmer for 2—3 minutes, until slightly thickened, and spoon over the ham.

Right: This roadside café is to be found in Twin Arrows. No doubt, its juicy steaks hit the mark!

At Seligman, the paths of the Old Road and I-40 diverge, with 66 heading northwest towards Peach Springs and then rejoining the Interstate (which continues more directly west) at Kingman. The first major attractions encountered on this loop of highway are the Grand Canyon Caverns, about 24 miles (39km) outside Seligman. Millions of years ago, these caves, which lie three-quarters of a mile (1,200m) underground, formed part of the bed of a huge ocean, but are now completely dry. Since their discovery in 1927, elevators, lights, and pathways have been installed inside, and regular guided tours are available.

Right: A tourist guide to the Grand Canyon Caverns dating from c. 1960.

NW ➡

Seligman

Peach Springs

1785

Grand Canyon Caverns

1820

66 now enters the Hualapai Indian Reservation en route for Peach Springs, a settlement 4,800 feet (1,460m) above sea level that is the headquarters of the Hualapai tribe, and was once the western terminus for the Santa Fe railroad. The town acquired its name after early settlers found peaches growing at a nearby waterhole; these may have originally been planted by Mormon missionaries.

Peach Springs

Truxton

From Peach Springs, Route 66 turns southwest toward Truxton, which lies just outside the Hualapai Reservation. The area was given its name by Naval Lieutenant Edward Beale, who visited this area in 1857 while surveying a wagon road from Arkansas to the Colorado River; Commodore Thomas Truxton was his maternal grandfather. In about 1900, a small Indian School was established at Truxton Canyon; however, the foundation of the town itself (which lies a few miles beyond the site of the school) is much more recent. It sprang from plans for a rail link to the Grand Canyon, which led

Above: An outbuilding used by the Indian school near Truxton — the school itself is on the right.

to a café and service station being opened in 1951 near the proposed site. The railroad never materialized, but the new ventures flourished, thanks to Route 66, and gradually a small community developed around them. Ray and Mildred Barker purchased the café from its original owner, Donald J. Dilts, in 1957, and Mrs. Barker still operates it today.

Left: An old drive-in restaurant sign, photographed near Truxton.

MUSIC OF THE ROAD →

In October 1998, English pub landlord Larry Sleight and seven of his friends — all members of a long-established amateur R & B band, The Quest — embarked on the journey of a lifetime. After arriving in Chicago and playing a gig for an audience of Route 66 devotees, the group boarded a 1954 scenic cruiser and headed down the highway to Los Angeles. They paused on the way to give a series of concerts, including one in Williams, Arizona — home of Paul Taylor, Publisher and Managing Editor of *Route 66 Magazine*, who had helped Larry arrange the trip. The band's US visit led to the setting up of the *Friends of Route 66 UK*, which is based in Larry's pub, the Drum Inn at Cockington, Devon. During February 1999, Paul and his family traveled to England to launch the new association — and enjoy more music from The Quest, who performed to celebrate the occasion.

Right: The Quest outside Route 66 Magazine's *headquarters in Williams.*

This plaque
The Frien
at The
by Paul,
from t
of

Saturda

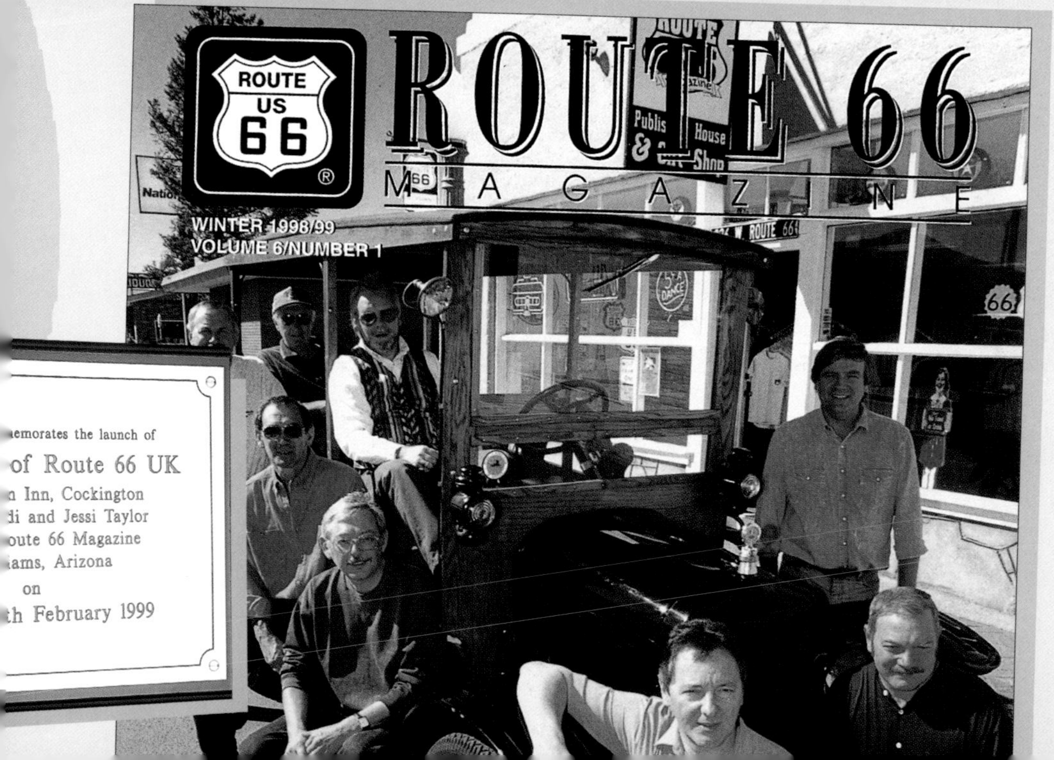

ROUTE US 66 ®

National

ROUTE 66

MAGAZINE

WINTER 1998/99
VOLUME 6/NUMBER 1

...memorates the launch of

...of Route 66 UK

...n Inn, Cockington

...di and Jessi Taylor

...oute 66 Magazine

...ams, Arizona

on

...th February 1999

The two remaining settlements on this section of 66 are Valentine, about 10 miles (16km) south of Truxton, and Hackberry, whose former General Store is now a Route 66 Visitor Center. The road then rejoins I-40 at Kingman.

Kingman took its name from Lewis Kingman, a locating engineer for the Atlantic and Pacific Railroad, around whose tracks it was formed in 1883. The town grew rapidly, acquiring big stores and other businesses, including the Beale Hotel — boyhood home of its most famous citizen, movie actor Andy Devine. 66 brought further prosperity to the town, and in the words of one commentator, the road is now "an essential part of Kingman's personality." The story of the city and the highway can be explored at the Powerhouse Visitor Center, headquarters of the Historic Route 66 Association of Arizona, and there are many other attractions for travelers to enjoy.

Left: A salutary warning to drivers heading west toward the Mojave Desert.

SW →

| 1870 | Oatman | 1929 | CALIFORNIA |

Kingman   1902   Topock

The last stretch of Route 66 in Arizona used to be the most hair-raising to travel. Beyond Kingman are steep gradients as the highway heads southwest towards the Black Mountains, where vehicles and drivers are faced with their ultimate challenge: the infamous Gold Hill grade. This climbs to the top of Sitgreaves Pass (3,515 feet [1,071m] above sea level) before snaking down to the little town of Oatman — a former gold mining center (now famous for the multitude of donkeys in its streets) where Clark Gable and Carole Lombard spent their wedding night after getting married in Kingman. After Oatman, 66 continues the remaining 27 miles (43km) towards the border settlement of Topock.

In 1951, this vertiginous route was bypassed by a new stretch of road (now part of I-40) that reaches Topock more quickly. However, the Old Road, and Oatman itself, are well worth making a detour to see before heading over the Colorado River into California.

Right: This old postcard shows the road between Kingman and Oatman in its pre-Route 66 days.

ON THE NATIONAL OLD TRAILS HIGHWAY — OCEAN TO OCEAN

HAIR-PIN CURVE, NATIONAL OLD TRAILS HIGHWAY, BETWEEN KINGMAN AND OATMAN, ARIZONA

The Electra Glide's name reflected the introduction in 1965 of an electric starter to the Panhead Duo Glide.

1965 Harley-Davidson
Electra Glide

Harley-Davidson's 1965 Electra Glide was the final incarnation of the classic Panhead engine design, which had been in continuous production since 1949, and was a familiar sight on America's highways. However, despite its success (nearly 7,000 Electra Glides were produced in 1965), it was being increasingly outsold by Honda and other Japanese machines.

Right: Other refinements to this version of the Panhead included a new frame and a bigger gas tank with a 5-gallon (8.9lit) capacity.

ROUTE
66

California

The town of Needles provides the Route 66 traveler's first real glimpse of California. The subsequent journey through the Mojave Desert towards Barstow was once a daunting prospect for drivers: the Joads, in John Steinbeck's *The Grapes of Wrath*, chose to cross it at night to avoid "[getting] the livin' Jesus burned outa us if we go in daylight." However, the road itself was a good one; by 1934, the entire, 320-mile (515km) stretch of Route 66 in California had been paved. After Barstow, the Joads turned off 66 for Bakersfield; however, the Mother Road continues via Victorville, San Bernadino, and Pasadena toward its ultimate destination: Santa Monica.

CALIFORNIA

Landscape & Climate

The Mojave Desert, west of Needles, may no longer pose the same threat to travelers as it did to the Joads and their real-life counterparts, but it remains a daunting, forbidding landscape, where temperatures approaching 100°F (38°C) are not uncommon. Beyond it lies the historic path over the Cajon Pass to San Bernadino (a city originally built by Mormon missionaries who had traveled across the desert from Utah), and the final stage of Route 66's journey — through land that was once full of citrus groves and livestock, but is now an almost unbroken urban sprawl leading to Los Angeles. However, the ocean shore at Santa Monica offers a chance to clear the smog from our lungs and relax at the end of the road.

"
If you ain't got that Do Re Mi boys
If you ain't got that Do Re Mi
Oh, you better go back to beautiful Texas
Oklahoma, Georgia, Kansas, Tennessee.
California's a garden of Eden
It's a paradise to live in or see
But believe it or not you won't find it so hot
If you ain't got the Do Re Mi.
"

(from Do Re Mi *by Woody Guthrie, 1937)*

Needles

1941

The town of Needles, named after the sharply pointed peaks of the nearby Mohave Mountain Range across the Colorado River, was established when the Southern Pacific Railroad arrived in the area in 1883. A satisfactory bridge to carry their tracks over the water was completed in 1890 (three earlier ones were swept away); and a road crossing for the Old Trails Highway (used by Route 66 until 1945) followed in 1916.

To travelers heading west on 66, the terrain on the far side of the bridge, described by John Steinbeck as a "broken rock wilderness," was a harsh introduction to the "Promised Land" of California. Needles itself must have seemed more welcoming — at any rate, for those with the "Do Re Mi" to enjoy facilities like the Harvey House or the numerous other lodging houses, some of which still survive. Others, forced to camp out or press on towards the Mojave Desert, might not have "found it so sweet."

Left: The Harvey House in Needles, dating from the 1930s, and (right) the 66 Motel, another Needles landmark.

dles ••• **1971** ••• Amboy

1941 ••• Goffs ••• **2018**

e next town on the original alignment of Route 66, was
e first places anywhere on the highway to be bypassed. In
ew, more direct road from Needles to Essex was
ced, dealing a deathblow to the little settlement. Recently,
though, its former schoolhouse (which closed in 1937) has become
the headquarters of the Mojave Desert Heritage and Cultural
Association, and it currently houses a unique collection of
photographs, books, and oral histories relating to the region.

Meanwhile, 66 continues south of the town, following the path of
the railroad tracks across the Mojave from Essex towards Amboy —
a tiny, once-derelict town now being rescued from its decline by two
new owners, Walt Wilson and Tim White. They acquired its ten
buildings (including Roy's Café and Motel) in 1995, and have
completely refurbished them, with an eye to attracting passing
visitors and tourists as well as film and TV location shoots.

Right: Only 300 miles to L.A...the highway stretches
west beyond Needles toward the Mojave Desert.

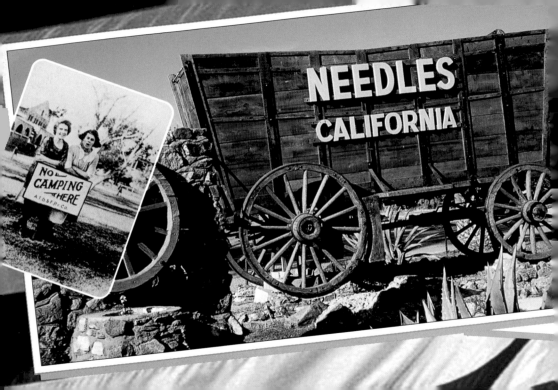

NEEDLES, CALIFORNIA

ROUTE 66

This old mule train wagon — a sharp reminder of how difficult road transportation was before the advent of automobiles and paved highways — can be seen at the eastern end of Needles' Broadway. Nearby are the rail tracks whose construction, in the 1880s, led to the birth of the city. This area of town was originally part of the campsite for the railroad workers — although later, as the inset picture shows, residents became more sensitive about where visitors pitched their tents!

Right: Barstow's railroad depot.

Just outside Amboy, the highway passes the crater of an extinct volcano, and continues through the desert via Bagdad towards Ludlow — where ore from nearby mines was once transferred to the main railroad line, and visitors to the town might still, as Bob Butcher put it in *Route 66 Magazine*, "hear the ghosts of hard rock miners... and workers from the Tonopah and

NW ➔

Amboy   2026   Ludlow   2080   Daggett   2102

2018   Bagdad   2047   Newberry Springs   2092   Barstow

Tidewater…swapping tall tales over the lunch counter." Beyond Ludlow lies Newberry Springs, location for the movie *Bagdad Café*, shot in 1987. The café featured in the film, originally called the Sidewinder, has since been renamed after the picture. After passing through Daggett, Route 66 now enters Barstow; named for the former president of the Santa Fe, William Barstow Strong, and once a major railroad center for the entire region. Sited at the junction of two key Interstates, I-40 and I-15, it remains an important staging post for today's road travelers.

Left: Members of the California Highway Patrol in Barstow in 1929, the year of the CHP's formation and (right) a Murphy Bros. sign in Ludlow.

East of Barstow, Route 66 used to lose a proportion of its traffic; in the 1930s, as Michael Wallis points out in his book on the Mother Road, "most Okies, including the Joad family, chose to continue west...and go to Bakersfield." 66 and I-15, however, turn southwest and head for Victorville — but by separate paths. While the modern Interstate follows a fairly straight line, the Old Road runs close to the Mojave River, taking in Lenwood, Helendale, and Oro Grande on its more leisurely journey.

Left: A road marker with a descriptive plaque, photographed at Helendale.

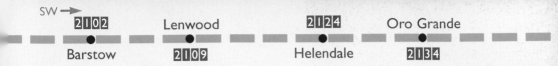

SW →
2102
Lenwood
2124
Oro Grande
Barstow
2109
Helendale
2134

The Oro Grande route had been familiar to travelers for hundreds of years. Early Spanish explorers, as well as 19th-century pioneers such as Jedediah Smith (who crossed the Mojave Desert in 1826—27) and the Mormons who traveled from Salt Lake City to build San Bernadino, all used it. Wagon trains and stagecoaches also passed through the area, which one historian has described as being "located at the historical crossroads of a great state."

Above: Bridge over the Mojave River at Oro Grande, c. 1932. The town has been an important river crossing for centuries.

The *Super Glide* combined *Electra Glide* frame with *Sportster* front end — it was aimed at customers who wanted a cruising bike with sporting flair.

1971 Harley-Davidson
FX Super Glide

The popularity of the American custom motorcycle scene was reflected (and boosted) by elements of the 1960s counterculture, and movies such as *Easy Rider* (1968) — much of which was shot on Route 66. More and more buyers were looking for machines like the specially customized "chopped hogs" ridden by Peter Fonda and Dennis Hopper; and Harley-Davidson's 1971 FX Super Glide was the first "factory custom" to offer them what they wanted.

VICTORVILLE CALIF

From Oro Grande, it is only a few miles to the bridge over the Mojave River that leads to Victorville, a high desert city (2,875 feet [876m] above sea level) with a fascinating history. It was once an important staging post on the early pioneers' pathway to the San Bernadino mountains; before being renamed for Jacob Nash Victor, construction superintendent on the California Southern Railroad, in 1885, it was known as Mormon Crossing. For a while, its main local industry was mining, but after the deposits were worked out, Victorville found new fame as a movie location; according to Bob Moore and Patrick Grauwels, more than 200 films were shot in the surrounding area between 1914 and 1937. It was especially associated with Westerns, and therefore a particularly appropriate place for the museum opened in 1976 by Roy Rogers, the "King of the Cowboys" (1911—1998). On the next two pages, we examine its attractions more closely.

Left: A postcard of downtown Victorville dating from the early 1940s. Route 66 passed through the town's 7th and "D" streets.

The Roy Rogers–Dale Evans Museum in Victorville is a treat for anyone with an interest in the Wild West on the big screen. The two stars were, of course, also husband and wife, and their respective steeds,

Trigger ("the smartest horse in the movies") and Buttermilk, can be seen preserved alongside hundreds of other exhibits reflecting every aspect of their careers. Roy himself had strong links with Route 66: born in Ohio, he made his first journey west on the Mother Road in 1930, driving from Missouri to California, and

suffering several flat tires and a major breakdown in New Mexico along the way. In an article for *Route 66 Magazine*, Dan Harlow describes how the King of the Cowboys "never forgot the highway that brought him to fame and fortune," and this is borne out by many of the photos and mementoes on display in the museum.

Left: Roadsign for the Roy Rogers—Dale Evans Museum — celebrating the movies' "King of the Cowboys," and the entrance to Victorville's Route 66 Museum (see page 393 for more details).

Did you ever hear tell of sweet Betsy from Pike

Who crossed the wide prairies with her lover Ike,

With two yoke of cattle and one spotted hog,

A tall shanghai rooster, and old yaller dog?

They soon reached the desert, where Betsy gave out,

And down in the sand she lay rollin' about.

While Ike in great wonder looked on in surprise,

Sayin' 'Betsy, get up! You'll get sand in your eyes.'

They swam the wide rivers and crossed the tall peaks,
And camped on the prairie for
weeks upon weeks,
Starvation and cholera and hard
work and slaughter,
They reached California spite
hell and high water.

(Old Pioneer Song)

The Old Road between Victorville and the Cajon Summit is now buried beneath the Interstate — and another memorable Route 66 institution, the Hulaville Museum, is also gone now. This eccentric but fascinating outdoor collection of bottles, signs, and other artifacts, fronted by a 15-foot model Hula dancer, used to be on display about five miles (8km) outside Victorville; it was run by a former carnival showman, Miles Mahan, who

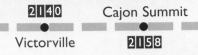

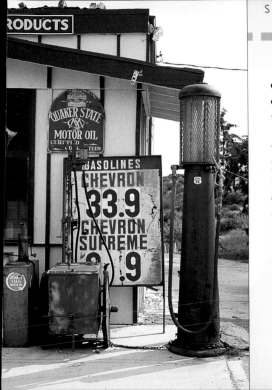

died in 1997. A few relics from his collection can still be seen in the town's California Route 66 Museum.

About 17 miles (27km) beyond Victorville, an exit leads off the highway towards the Cajon Summit itself — an elevation of 4,260 feet (1,298m). In pre-Interstate days, many drivers would have welcomed a rest stop here before embarking on the hair-raisingly steep descent into the San Bernadino Valley. Now, however, I-15 cuts through the Cajon Pass, making the downhill drive much safer — but rather less exciting.

Left: A vintage gas pump outside the Summit Inn's fuel station at Cajon Summit.

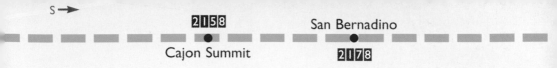

S →

2158
●
Cajon Summit

San Bernadino
●
2178

Having reached the bottom of the pass, I-15 branches off to the west, heading for San Diego. San Bernadino can be reached by bearing left onto I-215, and then following the path of 'Historic Route 66' into town. Originally the site of a mission settlement, modern San Bernadino owes its origins to the Mormons who crossed the Cajon Pass in 1851, and developed the new city over the following six years, before being summoned back to Utah by their Church's High Council. By the end of the century, San Bernadino was already a major center for commerce and transportation, and it has gone on to develop close links with the cities to its west; at one time, there was even a streetcar service connecting it with Santa Monica!

The Old Road now becomes SR66, and leads out of San Bernadino as Foothill Boulevard, taking in nearby settlements such as Rialto, site of the Wigwam Motel illustrated.

Left: The Wigwam Motel in Rialto, near San Bernadino, has been in business since 1950.

The Cheese 'n' Bacon Burger

MAKES 4 SERVINGS

Millions of hamburgers have been sold on Route 66 since its inception —
from the bagfuls of mini-burgers (20 for a dollar) offered by the White
Tower chain in the 1920s to the prime beef patties that feature on the
menus of top-class restaurants. No one can be sure when cheese, bacon,
and other now-traditional extras were first introduced, but they
provide a perfect complement to this all-American delicacy.

1 pound 12 ounces
ground beef

Salt and freshly ground
black pepper

8 slices bacon, cut in half

4 slices cheddar or
Monterey Jack cheese

4 burger buns, split
and toasted

Lettuce leaves, sliced
onion, ketchup,
mayonnaise, or other
favorite condiments,
to serve

1. Put the beef in a large bowl and season with salt and pepper. Mix and shape into 4 large patties. Refrigerate until ready to use.

2. Lay the bacon slices in a large, heavy-bottomed frying pan and set over medium-high heat. Cook for 5—8 minutes, until crisp, turning once. Remove the bacon to a paper towel to drain.

3. Pour off all but 2 tablespoons of the bacon drippings and return the pan to the heat. Add the hamburgers to the hot pan and cook for 6—8 minutes, or longer for more well-done burgers, turning once. One minute before the end of the cooking time, top each burger with a slice of cheese to soften.

4. Arrange the lettuce on the burger bun bottoms and transfer each burger to a lettuce-lined bun. Top each burger with 2 slices of bacon, sliced onion, ketchup, or any other condiments. Cover with the top of the bun and serve immediately. Serve with French fries.

*Left: The Café 50's in Santa
Monica, and it's time to eat.*

W →

2178

Fontana

2193

San Bernadino

2183

Rancho Cucamonga

Only about six miles (10km) from the Wigwam is another Route 66 institution: Bono's Restaurant and Deli, which has been serving up fine food for travelers since the 1930s. A little further west lie Fontana and then Rancho Cucamonga — whose name is derived from a Shoshonean Indian word meaning "sandy place." The community's origins back to 1833, when Tubercio Tapia acquired 13,000 acres (5,260ha) of land in the area from the Governor of Mexico. After building himself an impressive adobe residence there, Tapia first dedicated himself to raising cattle, and went on to establish the first winery in California six years later. Parts of the original buildings still survive, but wine is no longer made in the area, and several of the region's old wineries have now been converted into shopping centers and similar commercial utilities. Rancho Cucamonga (population 117,000) was officially incorporated as a city in 1977.

Right: A Route 66 institution — Bono's Restaurant and Deli between Rialto and Fontana.

A little way beyond Rancho Cucamonga is Upland, with its statue of the Madonna of the Trail — a pioneer woman with a baby in her arms, an older child clinging to her skirt, and a rifle in her hand. The statue, commissioned by the Daughters of the American Revolution in 1927, and designed by August Leimbach, is one of a series of 12 "Madonnas" displayed along the path of the National Old Trails Road.

Route 66, continuing down Foothill Boulevard, now enters Los Angeles County and the city of Claremont — especially notable as an academic center, with six colleges attended by a total of 5,000 students. Its oldest educational institution, Pomona College, dates from 1887.

Right: Upland's "Madonna of the Trail" statue — a tribute to the women who helped to settle the west.

MADONNA OF THE TRAIL

W ➡

Rancho Cucamonga 2196 Claremont 2200 Glendora 2208
2193 Upland 2198 La Verne 2205 Azusa

West of the nearby communities of La Verne and Glendora is Azusa, site of the Foothill Drive-In Theatre, one of the few surviving single-screen cinemas in this area: a long-time landmark on the Old Road, still attracting sizeable audiences.

Above: The exterior of the Foothill Drive-In Theatre in Asuza, which is still pulling in audiences on the Old Road.

1959 Chevrolet Corvette

From 1960 to 1964, Chevrolet co-sponsored the American TV show *route 66* (its title had no capital "R"). The series, comparatively little of which was actually filmed on the Mother Road, starred George Maharis, Marty Milner...and their Chevrolet Corvette roadster, which featured in every episode. Originally launched in 1953, the roadster had been restyled with fashionable "quad" double headlamps (as shown here) two years before the advent of *route 66*. Exposure on TV did wonders for the new model's sales, and it remained in production until 1962.

The Corvette roadster was a response by General Motors to the growing number of British open-topped sports cars — including MGs, Jaguars, and Austin-Healeys — finding favor with American drivers in the early 1950s.

Left: The concave side scoops were introduced in 1956.

Past the Drive-In Theatre (and the disused, old-style McDonald's just beyond it) the road enters Duarte — a place that takes its Route 66 heritage seriously. In 1996, the city held the first of its now-annual parades in honor of the Mother Road. Nearly 5,000 spectators attended the event, which featured vintage vehicles, marching bands, and colorful historical costumes; the guest of honor, Bobby Troup, led the celebrations from the back of a 1948 Buick convertible. The parade takes place every

Right: The Aztec Hotel in Monrovia, designed by Robert Stacy-Judd.

W ➜

Azusa   2210   Monrovia   2214   Pasadena
●   ●   ●   ●   ●
2208   Duarte   2212   Arcadia   2222

September; further information about it can be found on pages 390-393.

Just west of Duarte is Monrovia: the town dates from 1886, and among its most interesting and unusual buildings is the Aztec Hotel (on Foothill between Magnolia Avenue and Alta Vista), built in 1925, and famous not only for its architecture but also for the Art Deco mural that graces its foyer. Next, the highway passes through Arcadia before reaching the city of Pasadena.

Right: The distinctive emblem of the Automobile Club of Southern California.

Pasadena

2222

Originally part of the San Gabriel Mission, modern Pasadena took shape in the 1870s with an influx of wealthy settlers, who built themselves elegant homes and impressive civic amenities. Their

successors added to the area's architectural richness, and today, no less than 1,000 Pasadena properties are listed on the National Register of Historic Places. The city's attractions include its Playhouse, opened in 1917 — where Dustin Hoffman, Gene Hackman, and other fine actors began their careers; the Colorado Street Bridge, dating from 1913; and the mansions on

Above: Pasadena's elegant Colorado Street bridge — part of the city's historic downtown area.

1949
Pasadena

50c

TOURNAMENT
OF ROSES

Review

"Millionaires' Row" (Orange Grove Boulevard). One of these, the former home of a member of the Wrigley's Chewing Gum dynasty, is the headquarters for Pasadena's famous "Tournament of Roses" — first staged on New Year's Day 1890, and now held annually. At its heart is the Rose Parade, featuring flower-covered floats and marching bands, followed by a football game at the city's Rose Bowl; both events attract massive crowds and millions of TV viewers.

Come with me to the warm South

Or the gold Californian West...

Lutes we ain't got

But guitars a-plenty

(from Songs for Dov *by Michael Tippett, 1905–1998)*

Right: A limited edition Harley-Davidson Fender Stratocaster
with chromed body and gold-plated trim.

We have now reached the final stage of Route 66's journey from Chicago to the Pacific. Its path west from Pasadena towards Santa Monica leads through the sometimes glamorous, but often seedy, sprawl of Hollywood; it seems extraordinary that, as recently as the 1880s, this area was still almost exclusively farming land. Hollywood's founder, developer H.H. Wilcox, began to lay out streets and sell building lots there in 1886 (his wife gave the place its name); and the

Right: Hollywood's Capitol Records building resembles a stack of singles!

community they helped to create was formally
incorporated in 1903. Eight years later, the Nestor
company opened the first-ever Hollywood film

studio, and as the industry
grew, the locality became
the base for almost all of
America's greatest
production houses. By the 1950s and 1960s,
Hollywood was also attracting record labels,
sound studios, and other media businesses —
including Herb Alpert
and Jerry Moss's

A & M Records, which operated from a
distinctive headquarters on North Vine
Street, built in 1954.

*Above and right: Hollywood landmarks — the
Formosa Café and the Warner Brothers studio.*

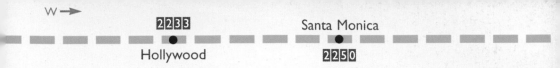

Beyond Hollywood, all that remains of Route 66 is a few miles of Santa Monica Boulevard, whose intersection with Ocean Boulevard marks the official end of the road. Nearby, in Palisades Park, is a plaque marking the dedication of "the Main Street of America" to Will Rogers in 1952, and a few blocks away is the famous Santa Monica Municipal Pier, built in 1909, and still one of the area's key attractions. Santa Monica itself is a long-established center for entertainment and leisure; some of its 1920s funfair-style facilities have recently been restored to their former glory, and its fine restaurants and elegant buildings add to its appeal. Devotees of Raymond Chandler thrillers visiting Santa Monica for the first time may feel they know the city already; it was the location for many of his stories, notably *Farewell My Lovely*.

Left: The entrance to the recently restored Santa Monica Pier, a few blocks from the end of Route 66.

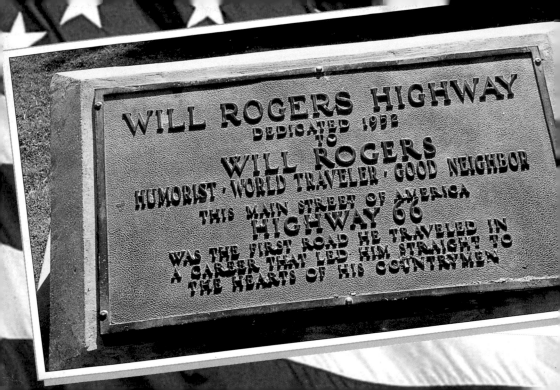

WILL ROGERS HIGHWAY
DEDICATED 1952
TO
WILL ROGERS
HUMORIST · WORLD TRAVELER · GOOD NEIGHBOR
THIS MAIN STREET OF AMERICA
HIGHWAY 66
WAS THE FIRST ROAD HE TRAVELED IN
A CAREER THAT LED HIM STRAIGHT TO
THE HEARTS OF HIS COUNTRYMEN

Will Rogers Highway Plaque

ROUTE 66

In 1952, Warner Brothers launched The Will Rogers Story, a movie based on the career of the Oklahoma-born star, who had died in a plane crash 17 years earlier. As part of the publicity for the picture, Warners and the Route 66 Association organized a convoy of vehicles that traveled down the highway to Santa Monica. There, at a ceremony in Palisades Park, this plaque was unveiled and the road dedicated to Rogers by Lyman Riley, President of the Missouri branch of the Association.

Epilogue

For the communities it passed through, Route 66 was a major artery, carrying the lifeblood of commerce and tourism. But within 20 years of its inauguration, parts of it were already under severe strain from a substantial growth in traffic; and as early as 1944, politicians and planners were considering the development of new highways to bypass its bottlenecks and accident black spots. These discussions remained largely theoretical until the 1950s, when President Eisenhower, who had been impressed by the autobahns he had seen in Germany during World War 2, set up a high-powered committee to look into the implementation of a similar road network for the USA. In 1956, after reading its report, Congress passed the Federal Aid Highway Act and the Highway Revenue Act: legislation that led to the construction of the Interstate system, and spelled the beginning of the end for Route 66.

During the 1960s, the new "superhighways" began to make their presence felt. Some had already been built, while disputes and delays surrounding others cast a long shadow over many towns and businesses on Route 66. The decline of the Old Road was gradual but inexorable: in the following years, more and more of it was bypassed, its distinctive signs were removed, and eventually — with the completion of I-40 near Williams, Arizona (see pages 310-311) — it became officially redundant.

However, it has refused to die. People from all over America — and far beyond — continue to relish its unique qualities: the extraordinary range of sights and scenes it offers, combined with a mixture of adventure, nostalgia, and romance that is as hard to define as it is to forget. As Paul Taylor puts it, "If folks tell you Route 66 is a passing thing like the hula-hoop…just smile!"

Bobby Troup

For Bobby Troup (1918—1999), Route 66 was, quite literally, the road to fame and fortune. Born in Harrisburg, Pennsylvania, he wrote his first hit song, *Daddy* (later recorded by Sammy Kaye) while still at college in his home state. After war service in the Marine Corps, Troup used his royalties to finance a move to California, sketching out lyrics and music for *Get Your Kicks on Route 66* during the 10-day westward drive on the Mother Road. The song, completed in 1946, was taken up by Nat King Cole, whose best-selling recording has been followed (to date) by almost 100 alternative versions.

Bobby Troup went on to write many other fine numbers (including several for his wife, singer and actress Julie London), and also became a successful film and TV performer; but *Route 66* remains his greatest achievement, serving (in Susan Croce Kelly's words) as "a musical road map for generations of westbound travelers."

Below: Bobby Troup with members of the English band The Quest in 1998.

BIBLIOGRAPHY

Basie, Count (with Murray, Albert): *Good Morning Blues* (Paladin, 1987)

Caughey, John Walton: *California* (Prentice-Hall, 1940)

Cooke, Alistair: *Alistair Cooke's America* (BBC, 1974)

Guthrie, Woody: *Bound for Glory* (E.P. Dutton & Co, 1943)

Hamons, Lucille: *Lucille: Mother of the Mother Road* (Cheryl Hamons Nowka, 1997)

Johnson, Paul: *A History of the American People* (HarperCollins, 1997)

Kelly, Susan Croce & Scott, Quinta: *Route 66 – The Highway and its People* (University of Oklahoma Press, 1988)

Kerouac, Jack: *On The Road* (The Viking Press, 1957, current edition Viking Penguin)

Mahnke, Dan: *Antique Roads of America, Bicycle Guide for Route 66* (Dan Mahnke, 1992)

Moore, Bob and Grauwels, Patrick: *Route 66 – The Illustrated Guidebook to the Mother Road* (Roadbook International, 1998)

Rittenhouse, Jack D.: *A Guide Book to Highway 66* (University of New Mexico Press facsimile edition, 1989)

Snyder, Tom: *The Route 66 Traveler's Guide and Roadside Companion* (St. Martin's Press, New York, 1995)

Steinbeck, John: *The Grapes of Wrath* (pub. 1939, current edition Viking Penguin)

Suttle, Howard: *Behind The Wheel...On Route 66* (Mass Market, 1996)
Wallis, Michael: *Route 66: The Mother Road* (St. Martin's Press, New York, 1990)
Ward, Geoffrey C.: *The West: An Illustrated History* (Little Brown & Co., 1996)
Ward, Greg (ed.): *USA — The Rough Guide* (The Rough Guides, 1994)
Witzel, Michael Karl: *Route 66 Remembered* (Motorbooks International, 1996)

MILEAGES

Because of the variety of alignments (some now abandoned) offered by Route 66 in its various stages of development and decline, it is almost impossible to arrive at definitive mileage figures for its length and for some city-to-city distances. Our measurements, giving a total of 2,250 miles from Chicago to Santa Monica, are based on a reasonably direct east-west journey via the more accessible and best-preserved sections of the Old Road. Some of the original alignments no longer survive, or are difficult to drive in a standard vehicle; thus we were, in places, obliged to use the Interstate, which generally takes a shorter, more direct path than Route 66.

ADDRESSES, INFORMATION, AND INTERNET LINKS

ROUTE 66: ORGANIZATIONS AND RESOURCES

National Historic Route 66 Federation

P.O. Box 423
Tujunga, CA 91043-0423
E-mail: *national66@national66.com*
www.national66.com

The largest Route 66 group in the world, founded in 1994, active in preservation projects, and offering membership (with many benefits, including a quarterly magazine and a Route 66 Lodging and Dining Guide) to supporters of the Mother Road in the USA and beyond.

"Historic Route 66"

route66.netvision.be/
Belgian-based site providing detailed descriptions of the road in all eight states.

Route 66 USA Ltd.

www.route66usa.com

Michael Wallis' Virtual Campfire

www.michaelwallis.com
Fascinating website run by the author of *Route 66: The Mother Road* (see Bibliography)

Route 66 Magazine

326 West Route 66
Williams,
AZ 86046

STATE-BY-STATE: ORGANIZATIONS AND RESOURCES

ILLINOIS
Route 66 Association of Illinois
2743 Veterans Parkway #166
Springfield, IL 62704
www.i66assoc.org/

MISSOURI
Route 66 Association of Missouri
P.O. Box 8117
St. Louis, MO 63156
www.missouri66.org

Meramec Caverns
(pages 80-81)
I-44 West, Exit 230
Stanton, MO
Open every day except
Thanksgiving & Christmas
www.americascave.com/

Trail of Tears State Park
(pages 88-89)
429 Moccasin Springs
Jackson, MO 63755
rosecity.net/tears/tears1.html

KANSAS
Kansas Route 66 Association
P.O. Box 169
Riverton, KS 66770

OKLAHOMA
Oklahoma Route 66 Association
P.O. Box 21382
Oklahoma City, OK 73156
www.nowka.com/ok66g.html

Will Rogers sites
(pages 144-147)
See the Will Rogers Official
Webpage at
www.willrogers.org/

National Cowboy Hall of Fame, Oklahoma City
(pages 166-167)
1700 NE 63rd Street
Oklahoma City, OK 73111
www.cowboyhalloffame.org/

National Route 66 Museum
(pages 172-173)
2229 W. Gary Blvd.
Clinton, OK
Winter opening hours
(September 1—April 30)
Monday—Saturday 9.00
am—5.00 pm
Sunday 1.00 pm—5.00 pm
(Summer hours differ —
check for details)
www.route66.org/

National Route 66 Museum
(pages 178-179)
P.O. Box 5
Elk City, OK 73648
Open Monday through
Saturday 9.00 am to 5.00 pm
Sunday 2.00 pm—5.00 pm
(closed on some holidays)
www.national66.com/elk_city/index.html

TEXAS
Old Route 66 Association of Texas
P.O. Box 66
McLean, TX 79057

University of Texas Handbook of Texas Online
www.tsha.utexas.edu/handbook/online/search.html

Shamrock (pages 191-195)
www.geocities.com/~shamrocktx/

NEW MEXICO
New Mexico Route 66 Association
1415 Central Avenue NE
Albuquerque, NM 81706
www.rt66nm.org/

Petroglyph National Monument (pages 260-261)
6001 Unser Boulevard NW
Albuquerque, NM 87120
www.desertusa.com/pnm/pnm.html

Ice Caves & El Morro
(pages 272-273)
Ice Caves:
www.icecaves.com
The Ice Caves can be reached from Exit 81 on I-40; walking trails and motor tours are available.

El Morro:
El Morro National Monument
Rt 2, Box 43
Ramah, NM 87321
The Visitor Center's daily summer opening hours are 9.00 am to 7.00 pm; self-guiding trails operate from 9.00 am—6.00 pm.
In winter, the Visitor Center is open from 9.00 am to 5.00 pm, and self-guiding trails are available from 9.00 am—4.00 pm. Closed December 25 and January 1.
www.nps.gov/elmo/

ARIZONA
Historic Route 66 Association of Arizona
P.O. Box 66
Kingman, AZ 86402
www.azrt66.com

Painted Desert/Petrified Forest (pages 292-293)
P.O. Box 2217
Petrified Forest National Park, AZ 86028
www.desertusa.com/pet/index.html
Exit 311 on I-40 leads through the park to the Painted Desert Visitor Center. The Rainbow Forest Museum is at the south end of the park, near the exit to US 180.

Meteor Crater (pages 304-305)
www.meteorcrater.com/
The Meteor Crater Visitors Center is open 365 days a year.
From May 15—September 15: 6.00 am—6.00 pm
Sept 16—May 14: 8.00 am—5.00 pm

Grand Canyon Railway from Williams (pages 314-315)
www.thegrandcanyon.com/gcr/index.htm

CALIFORNIA
California Historic Route 66 Association
2127 Foothill Boulevard #66
La Verne, CA 91750
wemweb.com/chr66a/index.html

Victorville (pages 352-355)
The Roy Rogers-Dale Evans Museum
15650 Seneca Road,
Victorville, CA 92392
Open daily 9.00 am—5.00 pm
The museum is closed on Christmas Day, Thanksgiving Day and Easter Sunday
www.royrogers.com/

California Route 66 Museum
P. O. Box 2151
Victorville, CA 92393.
The museum is open 10.00 am—4.00 pm Thursday—Monday, admission free
www.national66.com/victorville/index.html

Duarte Annual Parade (pages 372-373)
The City of Duarte's website (*www.ci.duarte.ca.us/city/*) includes a calendar of civic events, and provides advance notice of the date of its annual Parade (now combined with a picnic). Visitors are advised to check this website, or contact the City's offices, to obtain full details of each year's celebrations.

Picture Credits

Many of the photographs in this book are from Quadrillion Publising's own archive. The Route 66 memorabilia were photographed at Larry Sleight's Drum Inn in Cockington, Devon. Many thanks to him and the other contributors, whose assistance is gratefully acknowledged:

California Route 66 Museum/Dan Harlow: 242, 339, 346, 347, 349, 352, 352 (inset), 373.

Digital Vision: 16, 24-25, 37, 62-63, 66, 74-75, 80-81, 118, 126-127, 136, 144-145, 162-163, 186, 194-195, 218-219, 236, 244-245, 262-263, 286, 294-295, 300-301, 336, 344-345, 382-383.

Dan Harlow: 2, 9, 21 (insets), 24, 26, 28, 32, 38, 41, 42, 44, 45, 46, 50, 58, 61, 70, 73, 74, 79, 82, 83, 84, 89, 94, 95, 97, 108 both, 125, 126, 139 (inset), 141, 143, 146, 148, 152 lower left, 152-153, 156, 158, 162, 166, 170, 172, 173, 178, 181, 193, 194, 196, 197, 198, 203, 204, 208 left, 218, 222 (left inset), 230, 240, 243, 244, 246, 248, 252, 254 both, 259 (both insets), 260, 261, 262, 265, 266, 270, 273 (inset), 276, 278, 279, 290, 291, 294, 297, 298, 300, 302, 303, 304, 306-307, 308, 311, 316, 317, 318, 321, 322, 323, 324, 325, 328, 341, 343, 344, 346-347, 348, 354, 355, 357, 359, 360, 364, 367, 368, 369, 372, 374, 375, 378, 379 (all three), 380, 382.

National Historic Route 66 Federation: 88, 120, 140, 220.

Route 66 Magazine: 6, 11, 139, 144, 163 (inset), 183, 229 left, 239, 253, 269, 289, 305, 310, 331, 336, 340, 344 (inset),

Larry Sleight: 387.

Quotations Credits

Pages 18-19 and 306-307 *Route 66*, words and music by Bobby Troup. © Edwin H. Morris and Co Inc. and Burke and Van Heusen Inc., Warner/Chappell Music Ltd, London W6 8BS, reproduced by permission of IMP Ltd.

Pages 32-33, 40-41, 72-73, 114-115, 164-165, 220-221, 310-311 and 348-349 — extracts from *Route 66: The Mother Road* by Michael Wallis (St. Martin's Press) © 1990 Michael Wallis; used by kind permission of the author.

Pages 68-69 From *On The Road* by Jack Kerouac. © 1955, 1957 by Jack Kerouac; renewed © 1983 by Stella Kerouac, renewed © 1985 by Stella Kerouac and Jan Kerouac. Used by permission of Viking-Penguin, a division of Penguin Putnam Inc.

400 INDEX